CW01497172

© Danann Media Publishing Limited 2023

First published by Danann Media Publishing 2023

WARNING: For private domestic use only, any unauthorised copying, hiring, lending or public performance of this book is illegal.

CAT NO. SONO568

Cover design: Darren Grice
Book design: Alex Young
Editor: Martin Corteel
Proof reader: Finn O'Neill
Cover images: Getty Images
Photographs: All copyrights and trademarks are recognised and respected

All rights reserved. No part of this title may be reproduced or transmitted in any material form (including photocopying or storing it in any medium by electronic means and whether or not transiently or incidentally to some other use of this publication) without the written permission of the copyright owner, except in accordance with the provisions of the Copyright, Designs and Patents Act 1988. Applications for the copyright owner's written permission should be addressed to the publisher.

Original material reproduced by courtesy of Future Publishing 2023

© Future Publishing 2023

Not to be reproduced without permission.

Printed in E.U.

ISBN: 978-1-915343-27-7

This is an independent publication and it is unofficial and unauthorised and as such has no connection with the National Basketball Association (NBA) or any other organisation connected in any way whatsoever with the NBA featured in the book.

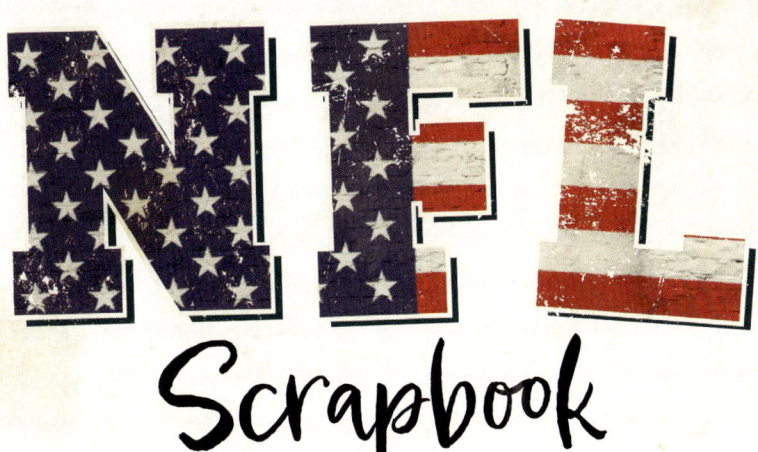

Scrapbook

sona
BOOKS

CONTENTS

INTRODUCTION

**W**hen the two teams left standing meet in the grand finale of each NFL season – the Super Bowl – the United States comes to a halt.

Tens of thousands of lucky ticket holders watch the game live. More than 100 million tune in to watch it on television. Millions more NFL fans around the world watch on their screens, often in the middle of the night. Some reside in countries that are hotbeds of support like the UK and Germany. Other live in fast-emerging, new markets like China. The half-time show is a sought-after entertainment slot that's featured Rihanna, Lady Gaga and Beyonce in recent years. Companies willingly pay $7 million for a 30-second TV ad.

The phenomenal interest in the Super Bowl arises from the fact that the NFL is one of the most popular sporting leagues in the world. It's a mix of physical strength and mental toughness with intricate skill and complex tactics. Wide receivers can run 40 metres in four seconds. Linemen can bench-press 100 kilograms without breaking a sweat. Cheerleaders and mascots entertain the crowd. Individual games often come down to the final play in the final seconds before a result is known. And the draft and salary cap ensure that no team dominates. At the start of every season, every fan can dream that their team has a genuine shot at making the Super Bowl, even if they had the worst record the season before.

Many of the sporting world's greatest athletes, coaches, teams and fixtures have contributed to the colourful world of American football. From Brady and Belichick to Bo and Joe, discover the colourful spectacle in these pages. One thing's for sure:

THE NFL IS NEVER DULL!

The States Air Force jets flying over the stadium during the singing of the National Anthem prior to the start of Super Bowl XLIII between the Pittsburgh Steelers and Arizona Cardinals

A BRIEF HISTORY OF THE NFL

The Greatest Show on Earth

The National Football League, or NFL, is the wealthiest sports league in the world by revenue. It has a higher average attendance of any sports league and includes teams that number among the richest in global sport. But the super-slick, professionalised game we know in the 21st century had humble origins. Come delve into the archives and discover the NFL's spectacular journey from Walter Camp to Patrick Mahomes.

Tom Brady drops back to pass for the New England Patriots - a common sight in the first two decades of the 21st century

HUMBLE BEGINNINGS

6 November 1869 is a date seared in NFL history. On that day, two college teams met for the first competitive game of American football – though a modern observer of the Rutger v Princeton fixture might think the game was an association football/rugby hybrid rather than American football. On that historic first meeting, the students played with a round ball and couldn't pick it up, only bat it with their hands. Play began with a scrum and scores were made by getting the ball into the opponent's goal. Over the next few years, the rules of the new sport were gradually codified and came to resemble modern-day football.

Handling was allowed, a line of scrimmage was introduced, and a snap began each play. But the new rules didn't do much to rein in the early game's brutality and violence. In 1905, President Theodore Roosevelt threatened to ban the game after 19 people died due to injuries incurred on the football field. The reforms that followed introduced a staple move of the modern game: the forward pass.

The professionalisation of American football began in 1892 when Pudge Heffelfinger was paid an eye-watering $500 to play for the Allegheny Athletic Association against the Pittsburgh Athletic Club. Perhaps it was a worthwhile sum to pay, because Allegheny won 4-0. The following week, Allegheny added a second pro, Ben Donnelly – but this time they lost. Heffelfinger and Donnelly were pioneer professionals, but they had to take their cash

Early footballers lacked protective pads and the game was notorious for its injuries and deaths

under the table. Pay-to-play was officially outlawed, but clubs got around the regulations relatively easily by offering players employment or gifting them watches and trophies that could be pawned for cash.

At the turn of the 20th century, football was organised on regional lines with few fixtures conducted outside state lines. The Ohio League was the stomping ground of Jim Thorpe, a double winner at the 1912 Olympics who was stripped of his gold medals for breaking the strict amateur code of the time. After being barred from track and field, Thorpe joined the Canton Bulldogs as a running back and helped his team to state titles in 1916, 1917 and 1919. Thanks to the growing popularity of stars like Thorpe, several entrepreneurial team owners began investigating the idea of a national championship. Some leagues banded together to create informal interstate circuits with teams travelling down the East Coast or the Great Lakes.

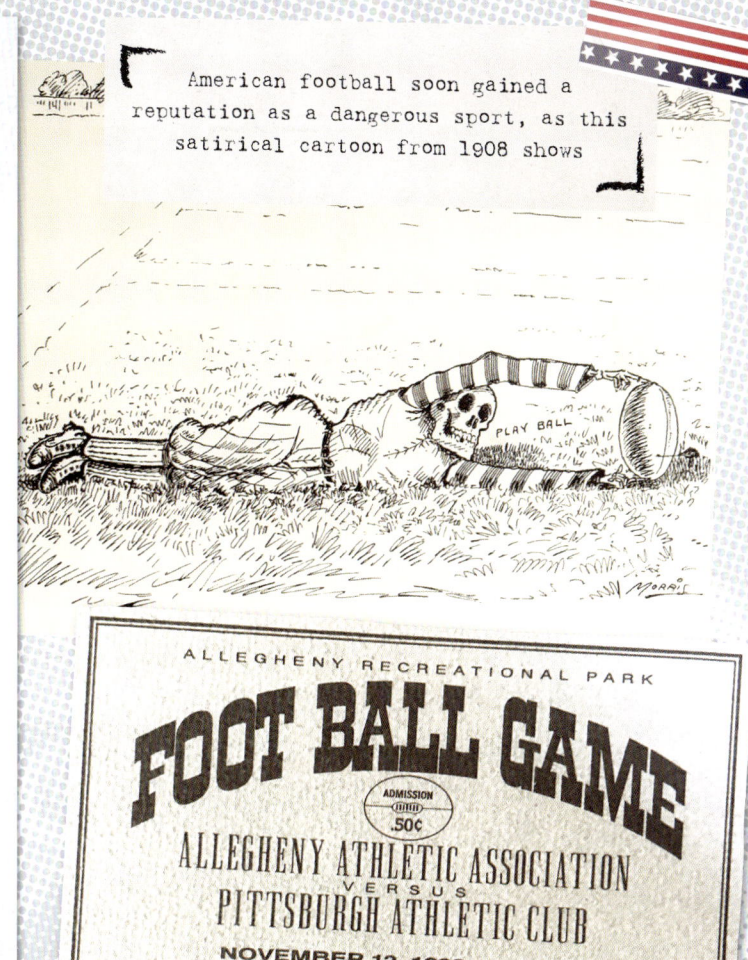

American football soon gained a reputation as a dangerous sport, as this satirical cartoon from 1908 shows

THE FATHER OF AMERICAN FOOTBALL

The sport of American football that Walter Camp played at Yale was a hotchpotch of rugby and football with rules that varied between colleges. When he returned to coach the Yale team, seven years after graduating, Camp helped to standardise the game's regulations. He dominated several rules committees and came up with proposals that made American football a recognisable, separate sport. Camp pioneered the line of scrimmage to replace contested scrums when a player was tackled, and the system of downs in which teams only have limited plays to move the ball forward.

Some contemporaries thought Walter Camp was too small to play football - but he soon made his mark off the field

BIRTH OF THE NFL

Deciding on an exact birthdate for the National Football League isn't easy. The forerunner of the NFL, the American Professional Football Conference, was founded on 20 August 1920 at a Hupmobile dealership in Canton, Ohio. One month later, on 17 September, the APFC was renamed the American Professional Football Association and teams from outside Ohio were added. Only on 24 June 1922 was the APFA renamed the National Football League.

Two current franchises took part in the inaugural season in 1920: the Chicago Cardinals (now the Arizona Cardinals) and the Decatur Staleys (now the Chicago Bears). But league membership was fluid. Teams came and went every season and owners happily moved cities in a search for the biggest fanbase and best grounds to play on. The first championships were decided on the best win-loss percentage since fixtures were as fluid as the teams making up the league. Some teams played games against non-NFL amateur and college teams and tried to claim those results towards the NFL

The Akron Pros won the first ever NFL Championship since they lost no games, although two other teams did win more due to playing more

The 1958 NFL Championship game boosted the NFL into the big time thanks to the close result and nationwide television coverage

championship. The Akron Pros were awarded the title in the first season with an 8-0-3 record, but the Decatur Staleys were miffed since they'd amassed more wins and ended the season 10-1-2.

There were inevitably a number of firsts during the early years of the NFL as owners, players and fans tried to figure out the best way to run the league. Eastern and Western Divisions were introduced in 1933 (by which point the NFL had dropped to just ten teams) with the two division winners playing off in an NFL Championship game for the first time. The Chicago Bears won that contest, beating the New York Giants 23-21. The first televised game was held on 22 October 1939, when the Philadelphia Eagles beat the Brooklyn Dodgers. Football also made it to the West Coast with the relocation of the Cleveland Rams to Los Angeles in 1945. That year also marked the last year of the NFL colour bar. Team owners had colluded to block black athletes from playing since 1934, but the newly relocated Rams broke ranks and signed African American running back Kenny Washington to prevent Californian lawyers taking action against the team's racist policies.

The first college draft was held in 1936, although it wasn't as heralded an event as the current NFL Draft because college football was actually more popular and drew bigger crowds than the professional game. Not until after the Second World War would the NFL finally surpass football's roots in the colleges. The point most historians pick as the NFL's breakthrough moment was the NFL Championship game in 1958, when the Baltimore Colts defeated the New York Giants in overtime. It was a perfect result for the first nationally televised game and has since been dubbed "the Greatest Game Ever Played". This stunning spectacle propelled the NFL into the big league – and it never looked back.

THE MERGER

By the end of the 1950s, the NFL was an undoubted success. The 12-team league expanded to 13 with the addition of the Dallas Cowboys in 1960 and 14 teams with the Minnesota Vikings in 1961. Tens of thousands of fans watched their favourite players every week, and most teams had moved to their own purpose-built football stadiums. But a group of wannabe franchise owners felt that expansion wasn't happening quickly enough, so they set up their own rival league – the American Football League – in 1960. It introduced football fans to a host of new teams that would soon become familiar names including the Boston (later New England) Patriots, Buffalo Bills and Denver Broncos.

NFL owners initially regarded the AFL as no threat. A long line of potential rivals to the NFL had previously been unveiled with fanfare, but each had quickly gone bust. But the AFL broke the mould. AFL owners were willing to challenge the NFL with its own college drafts and by offering competitive salaries. They won a high-profile signing when college quarterback Joe Namath elected to sign with the New York Jets of the AFL rather than the St Louis Cardinals of the NFL. In 1966, an informal agreement that neither league would poach each other's players was broken, and a free-for-all developed which led to soaring wages.

By June 1966, several NFL team owners decided to end the football war by combining the NFL

The AFL introduced two long-term rivals to the football world: the Boston Patriots and Buffalo Bills

and AFL. Both leagues committed to a common draft and an end-of-season championship game: the Super Bowl. In 1970, the leagues fully merged with two conferences – the AFC, predominantly comprised of former AFL teams, and the NFC, with mostly NFL teams. Although the league retained the National Football League name, several AFL innovations were adopted: an on-field game clock, names on player jerseys and revenue-sharing. Football became more of a nationwide sport too since the AFL had encouraged franchises in the South and encouraged black players to take up the game.

By the 1960s, NFL teams played in front of big crowds in purpose-built stadiums

SUPER BOWL I

The first Super Bowl was officially titled the World Championship Game, and it saw the Green Bay Packers take on the Kansas City Chiefs – the champions of the NFL and AFL respectively. Most expected the more established NFL team to beat their upstart rivals, and so it proved.

But the first half was closer than most people expected. The Chiefs offense gained more yards than their opponents and went into half-time within touching distance, down only 14-10. But the momentum shifted when a Packers safety intercepted a pass near the halfway line and returned it to the Chiefs' five-yard line. Green Bay quarterback Bart Starr then led his team to 21 unanswered

Bart Starr was named the first Super Bowl MVP - and he returned the following year to retain the title

points to complete a 35-10 win – a scoreline that perhaps flattered the winners. The AFL would have to wait a couple more years for its first Super Bowl title.

THE MODERN ERA

The AFC won its first Super Bowl in 1969 – the third edition of the revamped championship game – when the New York Jets defeated the Baltimore Colts. Few people gave the 11-3 Jets a chance before kick-off since the Colts had only lost once in the regular season. But they were led to a famous victory by quarterback Joe Namath – he who once signed a contract with the AFL that contributed to the league merger – and Namath famously quipped before Super Bowl III that he guaranteed a Jets victory. Few people believed him, but Namath lived up to his promise.

Namath is quite rightly regarded as the greatest Jet of all time thanks to his famous victory. Frankly, no player from succeeding Jets teams has come close to challenging him for the title. Super Bowl III remains the franchise's only NFL title – and their only Super Bowl appearance. But some teams enjoy a sustained period of success in the post-merger NFL. The Pittsburgh Steelers won four titles in the 1970s with Terry Bradshaw taking snaps at quarterback. The San Francisco 49ers were the team to beat in the 1980s. They matched the Steelers' record of four Super Bowl

Jerry Rice helped the San Francisco 49ers to four Super Bowl victories in the 1980s

'Broadway Joe' Namath led the shock of the century when the New York Jets became the first AFC team to with the Super Bowl

11 ENTER GATE X SECTION 61 ROW 45 SEAT

Third World Championship Game

SUNDAY, JANUARY 12, 1969 · 3:00 PM
ORANGE BOWL, MIAMI, FLA. $12.00
EST. PRICE $11.52 STATE TAX $.48 THIS TICKET CANNOT BE REFUNDED.

AFL-NFL WORLD CHAMPIONSHIP GAME
SUNDAY, JANUARY 12, 1969 · 3:00 PM
ORANGE BOWL, MIAMI, FLA. $12.00

wins in a decade with Jerry Rice catching passes from Joe Montana. The Washington Redskins, Miami Dolphins and Dallas Cowboys were perennial contenders too. Perhaps fearing that the game risked becoming too predictable and dominated by a small cadre of teams, the NFL introduced a salary cap in 1994. Initially, teams were allowed to spend $32 million on player salaries – a figure that would eventually rise to more than $200 million in 2022.

The post-merger era saw the NFL continue to innovate. Monday Night Football first aired on ABC in 1970 and proved enormously popular. On the field, new materials made helmets far more effective. But the NFL was forced to try new things because more rivals emerged, inspired by the success of the AFL. The World Football League started in 1974 and lured a few top players, including Larry Csonka and Paul Warfield from the unbeaten '74 Miami Dolphins. But the WFL folded due to financial problems and the Birmingham Vulcans and Memphis Southmen failed in their attempts to transfer to the NFL. The United States Football League did a little better. It lasted three seasons from 1983 to 1985 before it went bust.

And the NFL kept ringing the changes. It was a pioneer in adopting new technologies. In 1994, coaches were given the opportunity to communicate with players through in-helmet radios. Television viewers were given a treat in 1998 – a bright yellow line appeared on their screens indicating the target line teams were aiming for to get a first down. In 1999, on-field instant replays allowed officials to immediately check questionable calls.

But the NFL has never settled for the status quo. And even as the new millennium dawned, more changes were on the way.

INTO THE
21ST CENTURY

I n 2002, the NFL embarked on a realignment, inserting the Houston Texans as a new team and adding a South division in both conferences to make eight four-team divisions – the system still used today. But it didn't really matter which teams were in which divisions – the first two decades of the 21st century were the stomping ground of one dominant team: the New England Patriots. This underperforming franchise had never won the Super Bowl since it was admitted to the NFL in the NFL/AFL merger. But under head coach Bill Belichick and quarterback Tom

Brady, the Patriots won six Super Bowls in a 19-year period – and were the losing Super Bowl team on three other occasions. Despite such a phenomenal period of success, Brady still faced competition from some elite players. Peyton Manning was many people's choice for the greatest of all time until Brady's last two victories, while Patrick Mahomes made his debut for the Kansas City Chiefs in 2017.

America's most popular sports league had to endure more than its fair share of controversies after 2000.

A trip to a NFL stadium on game day is on the bucket list of many NFL fans around the world

Some came on the field, such as the New England Patriots being penalised for spying on opposing team's calls and deflating game balls. But others came off the field. The Washington Redskins opted to change their name in 2020 to avoid disrespecting America's indigenous people, eventually settling on the Commanders as an alternative. The impact of head injuries put the NFL under the microscope, with many claiming that the NFL could and should have done more to protect its players. And whether players should be allowed to kneel during the national anthem to protest against police brutality became such a hot issue that even President Trump joined the debate.

But despite the controversies, the NFL continues to expand and grow. With new superstars coming through the draft every year and new fans embracing the sport around the world, the future of the NFL looks rosy.

Bill Belichick's long coaching career has seen him lift the Lombardi Trophy on six occasions with the New England Patriots

INTERNATIONAL SERIES

In 1986, the NFL began a concerted effort to grow the sport that the rest of the world knew as American football. The American Bowl was a glorified preseason game held in London, Tokyo, Berlin and several other foreign venues over the next two decades. In 2005, the NFL began to schedule regular season games abroad. The first pitted the San Francisco 49ers against the Arizona Cardinals in Mexico City. Then London established itself as the NFL's most popular foreign outpost, with up to four games every season from 2007 (apart from when Covid-19 interrupted foreign travel). Now, the NFL aims to visit the UK, Mexico and Germany every year.

The Jacksonville Jaguars are regular visitors to London, where owner Shahid Khan also owns Fulham FC

TOP 10
LEGENDARY
NFL TEAMS

Every season sees a Super Bowl winner – but which teams would rise to the top if champions from one era faced another?

It's difficult to compare different teams from different ages... but that doesn't stop fans debating what would happen in a Vince Lombardi vs Bill Belichick match-up. Would the 1999 St Louis offense – the Greatest Show on Turf – be able to pierce the Steel Curtain defence of 1978 Pittsburgh? How would the 2007 Patriots do against the 1962 Packers, a team from their grandparents' generation? Here's our rundown of the top ten teams in NFL history.

The 1989 San Francisco 49ers recorded the fourth Super Bowl victory for Joe Montana - then an NFL record

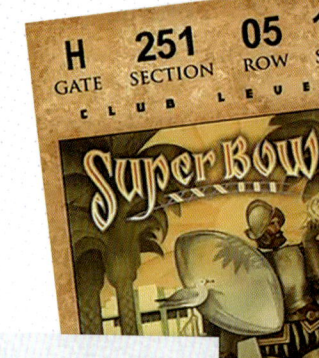

Elway's Last Dance
DENVER
BRONCOS
1998

The 1998 Broncos were a well-balanced team. Seven offensive players went to the Pro Bowl, and two defenders joined them. After a 14-2 regular season (the two losses coming late on when key players were rested), the Broncos progressed through the playoffs to Super Bowl XXXIII. And in the season finale, Denver recorded its second straight Super Bowl win thanks to the greatest player in franchise

history: quarterback John Elway, a player many thought was fated to never win the Super Bowl until he broke the curse in 1997. In 1998, Elway had a 99.2 rating in Superbowl XXXIII, where he passed for one touchdown and rushed for another and walked off the pitch as Super Bowl MVP. Then he walked away for good, going into retirement – although he later returned as Broncos general manager.

But although Elway was the crucial factor in the Super Bowl, his figures over the season showed a decline – perhaps no surprise for a quarterback in his 39th year. The Broncos actually made the NFL Championship game thanks to running back Terrell Davis, who rushed for 2,008 yards over the season – an average of 125 yards per game and five yards per carry.

John Elway scored a rushing touchdown in Super Bowl XXXIII after earlier launching an 80-yard touchdown pass

Versatile running back Paul Hornung was also responsible for kicking duties during his time with the Packers

Titletown Reigns
GREEN BAY
PACKERS
1962

Green Bay scored exactly 100 points over the first three games of the 1962 season. Even more impressively, they allowed just seven against them. And the Packers continued in much the same vein, living up to their tag as pre-season favourites to retain the NFL title they'd won the year before. They went 13-1 in the regular season, keeping their opponents off the scoreboard on three occasions.

Their only loss came to conference rivals Detroit Lions, but the Packers still topped the Western Conference and faced Eastern Conference winners the New York Giants in the NFL Championship game. They won that 16-7.

The 1962 Packers were so dominant thanks to their mean defence. It allowed an average of 10.8 points per game, and five defenders would later be enshrined in the Hall of Fame: defensive linemen Willie Davis and Henry Jordan, linebacker Ray Nitschke, cornerback Herb Adderley and safety Willie Wood. Two more Hall of Famers controlled the offense: Bart Starr led the league in passing yards and Jim Taylor led the league in rushing. Legendary head coach Vince Lombardi expertly marshalled his decent attack and stingy defence, meaning Green Bay had the NFL's best-ever points difference of +267 by the end of the season.

Monsters of the Midway

CHICAGO
BEARS

1985

The Bears were expected to be contenders at the start of the 1985 season, having lost to the 49ers in the previous year's NFC Championship game. But nobody expected them to win the Super Bowl in quite such style. They romped to a 15-1 regular season record. They obliterated the NFC Central, finishing eight games ahead of the Packers. They stormed to the Super Bowl, recording a 21-0 win against the Giants in the Divisional Round and 24-0 against the Rams in the NFC Championship. Then they smashed the Patriots 46-10 in Super Bowl XX, one of the most one-sided Super Bowls in history.

> The 1985 Bears were the first team to record back-to-back defensive shutouts in the playoffs

And they did it while maintaining a cool façade that was perfect for the MTV generation. Running back Walter Payton had a wide, toothy grin, but coach Mike Ditka had a permanent scowl. Quarterback Jim McMahon dazzled the media, as did rookie tackle William Perry, who embraced his 'Refrigerator' nickname.

The terrifying defence led the league, allowing only 198 points in 16 regular season games, and amassing 64 sacks and 34 interceptions. Offensively, Payton rushed for over 2,000 yards from scrimmage and scored nine touchdowns. Though the Bears didn't follow up on their success in future years and become a dynasty, the 1985 team had one of the best single-season performances in NFL history.

The Wowboys
DALLAS COWBOYS
1992

Some great teams have a stellar offense. Some have a smothering defence. The Cowboys of the early 1990s – and 1992 in particular – had both. They were a consistent scoring machine with the second-highest points total over the season. Quarterback Troy Aikman could select from a multitude of options: running back Emmitt Smith, wide receiver Michael Irvin, tight end Jay Novacek. No surprise that six offensive players made it to the Pro Bowl. But it was a huge shock that no defensive players joined them – because the Dallas defence ground down opponents across the pitch and allowed the fewest points against. Stars on this side of the ball included rookie safety Charles Woodson and defensive end Charles Haley.

The season started well with victories over the Washington Redskins and New York Giants – the two previous Super Bowl winners. Although the Cowboys subsequently lost three regular season games, they still secured the NFC East. After that, they blew away allcomers in the playoffs. Divisional rivals Philadelphia Eagles were first to fall, then the fancied San Francisco 49ers. In Super Bowl XXVII, the Buffalo Bills were embarrassed 52-17. It was the first of three titles in four seasons for the Wowboys.

SEC **116** ROW **22** SEAT **107**

GAME 4

1992 DALLAS COWBOYS
COWBOYS VS. REDSKINS
1992 DALLAS COWBOYS

Quarterback Troy Aikman spent his entire career in Dallas and won three Super Bowl rings

NEW ENGLAND PATRIOTS

2007

The Patriots were already a dynasty by the time the 2007 team hit the field. Head coach Bill Belichick had moulded a superb team around quarterback Tom Brady, and the two of them won the Super Bowl in 2001, 2003 and 2004. They'd go on to win three more in 2014, 2016 and 2018. But this particular Patriots team probably topped them all – despite not matching their achievement in winning the Super Bowl.

The 2007 Patriots raced to a perfect 16-0 regular season with a stunning offense. The next highest-scoring team languished 134 points behind, and the Patriots plastered more than 50 points against Washington and Buffalo. Brady threw a then-record 50 touchdown passes, and new receiver Randy Moss had 23 touchdown receptions.

Unfortunately for the Patriots, they came up against an in-form but streaky New York Giants team in the Super Bowl. The Giants were only in the playoffs thanks to a wildcard and benefited from a huge stroke of luck when receiver David Tyree caught a pass by clasping it against his head during a fourth-quarter drive. It went down in NFL history as the "Helmet Catch", ensured that Tyree would never have to pay for a drink in New York again, and spoiled the 2007's Patriots claim to be the undisputed greatest team of all time.

Tom Brady earned his first MVP selection thanks to New England's hot offense in 2007

The Surprise Package

WASHINGTON
REDSKINS
1991

Gary Clark was one of two Redskins with more than 1,000 receiving yards in 1991 – the other was Art Monk

The Redskins were a force to be reckoned with in the 1980s. But by 1991, with the majority of players had moved on and Washington were thought to be past their best. Then the 1991 team proved there was life in the old Skins yet. Despite lacking any real star names – cornerback Darrell Green and receiver Art Monk are the only players in the Pro Football Hall of Fame – the Redskins came through a tough NFC East that featured the Dallas Cowboys (who'd win the Super Bowl the following year) and the New York Giants (who'd won the previous year). The Redskins finished the regular season 14-2 – the two defeats were by narrow margins – and cruised through the playoffs, defeating the Falcons, Lions and Bills by a cumulative score of 101-41.

Statistically, this team was one of the best. The league-leading offense scored 485 points, almost 60 per cent above the league average. The defence was the second-best in the league. The turnover differential was an impressive +18. In an era when fans demand franchise quarterback and blue-chip players, the 1991 Redskins prove that a team is sometimes greater than the sum of its parts.

The Steel Curtain didn't allow a single first-quarter touchdown in the regular season

The Steel Curtain
PITTSBURGH STEELERS
1978

The Steelers were the dominant franchise of the 1970s. Chuck Noll's team topped the AFC Central every year from 1974 and won the Super Bowl in 1974 and 1978. Their success came thanks to a tough defence nicknamed the Steel Curtain, and it was so effective that the NFL enacted rule changes for the 1978 season to give opposition offenses a chance. The Mel Blount Rule, named after the physical Steelers cornerback, outlawed contact five yards from the line of scrimmage, and offensive linemen were allowed to use their hands to block pass rushers. But changing the regulations did little to stop Steeler dominance. They actually got better. Blount quickly adjusted still picked up four interceptions, while speedy wide receivers John Stallworth and Lynn Swann turned the no-contact rule to their advantage, helping to balance up the Steelers' lopsided, defensive gameplan.

Ultimately, the Steelers started the season with seven wins in a row and ended the regular season with a 14-2 record. Hall of Fame quarterback Terry Bradshaw had his best year and guided the Steelers to victory in an offensive shootout against the Cowboys in Super Bowl XIII, a fitting end to Bradshaw's MVP season.

The Greatest Show on Turf

ST LOUIS RAMS

1999

The 1999 Rams were all about the attack. Offensive coordinator (and future head coach) Mike Martz wanted his team to sling the ball, often employing five receivers on deep runs. Martz initially intended to launch his air raids through former Redskin quarterback Trent Green, who signed for the Rams in free agency. But Martz's plans came crashing down when Green went down with a torn ACL in preseason. That left the Rams in the hands of Kurt Warner, a career backup who's most recent experience was with the Amsterdam Admirals in NFL Europe and the Iowa Barnstormers in the Arena Football League.

But Warner was up to the task. He led the league in passing touchdowns, completions and passer rating. He was named league MVP and, after defeating the Tennessee Titans in a classic Super Bowl, Super Bowl MVP too. Warner was ably assisted by running back Marshall Faulk, the Offensive Player of the Year, and receiver Torry Holt, the Rookie of the Year. Together they led the NFL in scoring, putting 30 points or more on the board on 12 different occasions. Fans may have dubbed them the Greatest Show of Turf, but defences thought they were a nightmare.

Kurt Warner and Marshall Faulk led one of the most potent offenses ever seen in the NFL

75 ROW   81 SEAT

JARY 21, 1979

ONSHIP GAME
Kickoff 4:00 PM.
orida $30.00

SECTION Z

The Dynasty at its Best

SAN FRANCISCO 49ERS

1989

The 49ers were a dynasty in the 1980s, winning four Super Bowls – and the final team of the decade was perhaps the finest. Jerry Rice, the greatest wide receiver in the game, had one of his best seasons. He led the league in receiving yards (1,483) and touchdowns (17). Joe Montana had the best season of any quarterback in NFL history to that point. He had a passer rating of 112.4, a completion percentage of 70.2, and a 26-8 touchdown-interception ratio. In the playoffs, he got even better: 11 touchdowns to no interceptions. It was the yardstick by which future Hall of Famers like Payton Manning and Tom Brady were measured.

Perhaps surprisingly, two losses in the 14-2 regular season both came at Candlestick Park. The Los Angeles Rams squeezed to a one-point win, and the Green Bay Packers recorded a shock victory. But the 49ers still finished clear atop the NFC West, then knocked off the third-seed Minnesota Vikings in the playoffs. The NFC Championship saw the 49ers get revenge against the Rams, and the Denver Broncos were simply no match in Super Bowl XXIV. The 49ers outscored the Broncos by eight touchdowns to one in a 55-10 blowout.

The 1989 49ers had the greatest wide receiver in NFL history: Jerry Rice

LOGE

A NORTH GATE | 342 SECTION | 11 ROW

AFC-NFC World Championshi
Sunday, January 28, 1990 · 4:00
Superdome · New Orleans $125

SUPER BOWL X

28, 1990 · Gate
Superdome · Ne
00 All Taxes Inc

CTION
42

LOGE

Head coach Don Shula had two capable quarterbacks in Bob Griese (12) and Earl Morrall (15)

Undefeated

MIAMI

DOLPHINS

1972

Every season, when the last-remaining undefeated team loses its first game, the alumni of the 1972 Dolphins pop the champagne and toast the fact that their record has lasted another year – because the Dolphins of '72 are the only team to have gone through an entire regular season and postseason without losing. They amassed a 14-0 record in the regular season, then defeated the Browns, the Steelers and the Redskins to lift the Lombardi Trophy.

Even more impressive is that they did most of it without starting quarterback Bob Griese, who broke his ankle in the week five matchup against the San Diego Chargers. But backup Earl Morrall stepped into the breach, ensuring that the Dolphins beat the Chargers 24-10, before guiding his team to victory after victory. Morrall was harshly benched in the AFC Championship game and Griese returned to quarterback his team to win the Super Bowl 14-7.

It's true to say that the 1972 Dolphins had a relatively easy regular season schedule. But as the old adage says, you can only beat the team in front of you, and the Dolphins did that with aplomb, leading the NFL in both points scored and fewest points allowed.

Tom Brady of the New England
Patriots and Peyton Manning
of the Denver Broncos -
two legends of the game

LEGENDS
OF THE NFL

Every NFL game day, 53 players suit up for every NFL team. That adds up to a lot of players. The stats geeks at the NFL reckon that more than 25,000 men have played at least one snap in the NFL. Of those, around 300 have been deemed good enough to be elected to the Hall of Fame. But only 50 are good enough to make our exclusive list. Here are the legendary players who will live on as NFL immortals.

THE
HUMBLE HERO

No occasion was too big for Jerry Rice, the dominant wide receiver who captured three Super Bowl rings and fans' hearts alike

JERRY RICE

POSITION: Wide Receiver
NFL DRAFT: 1985/Round 1/Pick 16
CAREER: San Francisco 49ers (1985-2000)
Oakland Raiders (2001-2004)
Seattle Seahawks (2004)

••••

HIGHLIGHTS:
3 x Super Bowl Champion
(XXIII, XXIV, XXIX)
Super Bowl MVP (XXIII)
13 x Pro Bowl
(1986-1996, 1998, 2002)
2 x Offensive Player of The Year (1987, 1993)
NFL 75th Anniversary
All-Time Team
NFL 1980s All-Decade Team
NFL 1990s All-Decade Team
1,549 Career Receptions
(1st All-Time)
22,895 Career Receiving Yards
(1st All-Time)
197 Career Receiving
Touchdowns (1st All-Time)
Pro Football Hall Of Fame
(Enshrined 2010)

Jerry Rice   WR

NFL fans are obsessed with GOATs. That is, those who can lay claim to being the Greatest Of All Time. One name which is inescapable in such conversations is Jerry Rice.

When it comes to Flash 80, as he was affectionately known, fans usually dwell on the stats. Over a 20-year playing career, with the San Francisco 49ers,

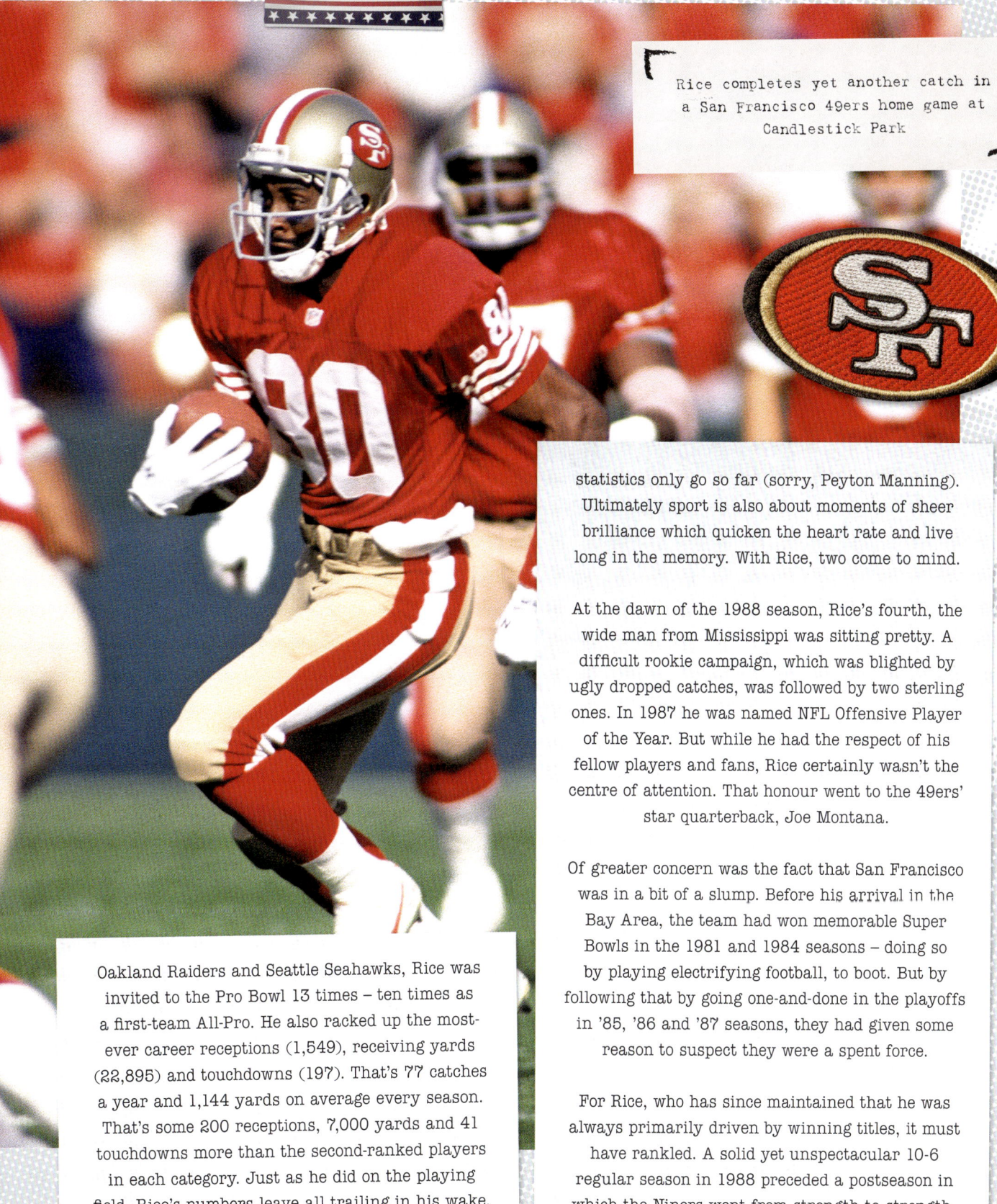

statistics only go so far (sorry, Peyton Manning). Ultimately sport is also about moments of sheer brilliance which quicken the heart rate and live long in the memory. With Rice, two come to mind.

At the dawn of the 1988 season, Rice's fourth, the wide man from Mississippi was sitting pretty. A difficult rookie campaign, which was blighted by ugly dropped catches, was followed by two sterling ones. In 1987 he was named NFL Offensive Player of the Year. But while he had the respect of his fellow players and fans, Rice certainly wasn't the centre of attention. That honour went to the 49ers' star quarterback, Joe Montana.

Of greater concern was the fact that San Francisco was in a bit of a slump. Before his arrival in the Bay Area, the team had won memorable Super Bowls in the 1981 and 1984 seasons – doing so by playing electrifying football, to boot. But by following that by going one-and-done in the playoffs in '85, '86 and '87 seasons, they had given some reason to suspect they were a spent force.

For Rice, who has since maintained that he was always primarily driven by winning titles, it must have rankled. A solid yet unspectacular 10-6 regular season in 1988 preceded a postseason in which the Niners went from strength to strength, blowing out the Minnesota Vikings, before scoring 28 points against the Chicago Bears' fêted defence.

Oakland Raiders and Seattle Seahawks, Rice was invited to the Pro Bowl 13 times – ten times as a first-team All-Pro. He also racked up the most-ever career receptions (1,549), receiving yards (22,895) and touchdowns (197). That's 77 catches a year and 1,144 yards on average every season. That's some 200 receptions, 7,000 yards and 41 touchdowns more than the second-ranked players in each category. Just as he did on the playing field, Rice's numbers leave all trailing in his wake.

But to speak only of numbers is to miss the point. After all, in the pantheon of sporting greatness,

Jerry Rice being introduced as an Oakland Raider in June 2001 by head coach Jon Gruden

But Super Bowl XXIII, against the Cincinnati Bengals, was a different prospect entirely. A stinker for all but the last three minutes, it was redeemed by what may well be the greatest championship-winning drive in NFL history. And it was the only one of San Francisco's five championships which went down to the wire.

But for Rice, it could have been all over before it even started. A week before Super Bowl Sunday, he rolled his ankle during practice, causing a flare-up of an injury he'd struggled with for months. But he was not to be denied.

Rice caught 11 of his team's 23 total receptions, for 215 of their 357 receiving yards. The former was a record until 2017 – and the latter still is. He also notched a touchdown. In other words, had Rice even enjoyed a regular day at the office, the 49ers would not have won the Super Bowl.

But football is not about numbers alone. As San Francisco's go-to receiver, Cincy's defensive backs did everything they could to stop him. His 11 catches came largely with a forest of arms flailing in his face, and he faced double coverage most of the day. The true test of a player is whether they can deliver in the clutch. With 3:20 left on the clock, the Niners started their final drive at their eight-yard line, trailing 16-13.

Of his two plays on the game-winning drive, Rice's most memorable was his final act of the day. On second down and 20, on the Bengals' 45 yard line, Montana went all-or-nothing to connect with the double-covered Rice. His route had to be perfect. The ball was in the air for 13 yards – not enough for a first down with time ticking. Rice grabbed it in the middle of the field amid a pack of Bengals, but ran for another 14, bringing it inside field goal range.

Bengals cornerback Lewis Billups later said: "It had to be a perfect throw and catch. He had all kinds of hands flashing in front of him." From there, with under a minute left, Montana connected with John Taylor in the end zone, and the rest is history.

The measure of Rice's performance, both in production and in cold-blooded clutch-ness, is probably summed up by the fact that San Francisco's quarterback made 23 of 36 pass attempts for 357 yards and two touchdowns, and yet no-one in Miami's Joe Robbie Stadium that night begrudged Rice's Super Bowl MVP

The wide receiver takes to the field in November 1988 – the season of his first Super Bowl title

award. Or, you could just listen to Cincinnati's safety David Fulcher, who said he felt his secondary "didn't do a bad job on him... He only scored one touchdown."

Rice is also credited with revolutionising the wide receiver position. Pass-first offenses may be the norm today, but the NFL of the 1980s almost looked like a different sport. Although it was developed by San Diego Chargers head coach Don Coryell, Bill Walsh's San Francisco 49ers were the first team to enjoy era-defining success with a true 'vertical passing' style. And a new system needed new types of players. Niners quarterbacks Montana and Steve Young have spoken of enjoying an almost telepathic understanding with Rice. Quarterbacks always knew exactly where their star receiver would be at all times.

Young, San Francisco's starting QB between 1991 and 1999, said: "The way he moved was somehow predictable, and he really made it easy for me to throw the football. He was just so consistent in his motion and movement that I always knew where he was going to be."

The other way he changed his sport was in his play after the catch. Never the quickest guy on the field, Rice wasn't known for torching defensive backs over the top. Instead, his forte was his hustle and desire to move the chains through sheer force of will. In fact, Jon Gruden, who was Rice's head coach in Oakland and a coaching assistant with the 49ers in 1990, described him as the greatest-ever wide man in terms of maximising yards gained after the catch. Fastidious to a fault, he was less an artist than a craftsman. His unparalleled attention to detail meant that he squeezed every last drop of talent from his body. No energy was wasted.

Teammates recall how he seemed faster with pads on than without. It's easy to see why. Hours of preparation made him perhaps the athlete most finely-tuned to NFL football in league history. He looked like he was born to play. Ronnie Lott, Rice's Niners teammate for five years, recalled the wide receiver's "insatiable appetite to get an edge and be the best".

Former 49ers owner Eddie DeBartolo went one further, saying that Rice personified the concept of professionalism. "I've never seen a player more driven or willing to work harder to become the greatest of all time," he once said. Many would argue he succeeded.

Jerry Rice of the San Francisco 49ers carries the ball against the Tampa Bay Buccaneers, December 19, 1992

FROM CATCHING BRICKS TO FOOTBALLS

Jerry Rice's famously supple hands, which helped him to wrangle more than 1,500 career passes and three Lombardi trophies, were the product of an unusual training regime. During long working days in the Mississippi sun as a boy, Rice mastered his craft by catching bricks being thrown to the ground by his brick mason father.

And the young man's speed and hustle were the product of hours of chasing horses – the only way he would get to ride them – which would sometimes take up to an hour to run down.

"He handled bricks better than any worker I ever had," his father, Joe, told Sports Illustrated. "I was sorry to see him go." The story of Rice's formative days as a farm-hand has followed him around for years, becoming the stuff of legend. The man himself explained: "There were horses you had to catch and sometimes it would take 45 minutes to an hour to run them down. During the summer my father would take me to work with him.

"My brother and I, we had developed this technique where you throw the bricks up, they were separated, and I was snatching them in the air. So the myth about me learning to catch footballs from catching bricks, that's where it came from."

"Quarterbacks always knew exactly where their star receiver would be at all times"

A GATE NORTH | 342 SECTION | 11 ROW | 09 SEA

AFC-NFC World Championship Gam
Sunday, January 28, 1990 • 4:00 PM
Superdome • New Orleans $125.00

SUPER BOWL XXIV

Sunday, January 28, 1990 • Gates Open 1:00

SEA
09

Rice during a 1992 game against the Arizona Cardinals at Sun Devil Stadium in Tempe, Arizona

Jerry Rice, the Super Bowl XXIII MVP in 1988, caught 11 passes for 215 yards on the day as the San Francisco 49ers downed the Cincinnati Bengals

While other players of his standing might have headed in for an early shower after practice, the future Hall of Famer wanted to get perfectly used to the new angle Young would be throwing at. That's because for most players, winning just one Super Bowl is the pinnacle. And two would be like winning the lottery. But Rice was never 'most players'. On claiming the Lombardi trophy, Rice said: "For a moment, you're in that locker room. We just played on the biggest stage and won a championship. Then, all of a sudden you start thinking 'Okay, we've got to come back next year and do it'."

During the Niners' four championship-less years – between 1990 and 1993 – the Dallas Cowboys had the measure of the California team, inflicting painful defeats in the '92 and '93 NFC Championship games. Some wondered whether the dynasty was over. Young has, on more than one occasion, called it 'the monkey on his back'.

After overhauling its defense, the Niners' redemption came in the form of a 38-28 win over the arch nemesis Cowboys in the NFC title game at San Francisco's Candlestick Park. Back in

Success in the 1988 season was followed up with another title a year later, in one of the most lopsided Super Bowls ever, a 55-10 blowout of the Denver Broncos in New Orleans. But during the peak of Rice's career, the Niners went through a relative drought, struggling initially with Young's succession of Montana. Number 80 refused to allow his focus to dim. When the left-handed Young officially took over from 'Joe Cool', Rice spent hours on the practice field catching lefty balls, demanding that the unfortunate Ted Walsh, an assistant coach, to put as much zip on the ball as Young.

Miami, San Francisco had to finish the job against plucky underdogs in the San Diego Chargers.

But San Diego's day looked doomed just three plays in, with Young tossing a 44-yard touchdown bomb to Rice. He would go on to make two more scores in a performance some have labelled his greatest ever. Although he didn't win the game's MVP award – which deservedly went to Young for his six-touchdown day – Rice was simply unplayable that day. He caught ten balls for 149 yards and three scores. Rather than retiring, Rice continued with the Niners until 2000, and then spent four seasons in Oakland, where he twice topped the 1,000 yard mark for the season, before a one-season hurrah with the Seattle Seahawks. He was inducted into the Pro Football Hall of Fame in 2010, in his first year of eligibility, and the Niners retired his No. 80 jersey the same year.

Art Spander, who has covered Bay Area sports for the San Francisco Examiner since 1965, marked out Rice's ability to perform in the clutch above all his other attributes.

Spander said: "His immediate start was troublesome – he dropped passes, which led to tears. Then he caught everything, anywhere, and especially in big games. He just kept scoring." Aside from apparently crashing an average of one wedding each week (look it up), Rice keeps a relatively low-profile these days.

His name, however, seldom goes unmentioned in GOAT debates to this day. In 1999 he was ranked second in the Sporting News' 100 Greatest Football Players, and topped a 2010 NFL Network poll of the league's best-ever player. Most fans, fellow players and pundits rank him as the best wide receiver to ever lace up a pair of cleats.

And perhaps the greatest part of the Jerry Rice story is that his mix of doggedness and determination was just as important to his success as his God-given ability. As he once remarked: "There was no way I was going to be denied. I kept working hard and my dream came true. I tell kids 'Do not let any obstacles stand in your way. If you want to achieve something, go for it. I'm living proof'."

Rice, left, and quarterback Joe Montana, after the 49ers' victory over the Denver Broncos in Super Bowl XXIV

Jerry Rice caught up with former 49ers quarterback Joe Montana on the sideline at Super Bowl 50

Jerry Rice with his bust during the 2010 Pro Football Hall of Fame Enshrinement Ceremony

MAESTRO OF MAYHEM

"I wouldn't ever set out to hurt anyone deliberately unless it was important – like a league game."

DICK BUTKUS

POSITION: Middle Linebacker
NFL DRAFT: 1965/Round 1/Pick 3
CAREER: Chicago Bears (1965-1973)
••••
HIGHLIGHTS:
8 x Pro Bowl (1965-72)
2 x NFL Defensive Player of the Year (1969, 1970)
NFL 75th Anniversary All-Time Team
22 Career Interceptions
25 Career Fumble Recoveries
Pro Football Hall of Fame (Enshrined 1979)

When they say All-Pro middle linebacker," the Chicago Bears standout once remarked, "I want them to mean Butkus." Who is the best at any position is always case for debate. But when mentioning premium middle linebackers, Dick Butkus is always at or near the top of every list.

Consumed with the idea of being the best, he played every game as if it were his last and no-one played with more intensity. His nine years with the Bears earned him All-Pro recognition seven times, as well as eight Pro Bowl invitations.

A two-time All-American at Illinois, Butkus was drafted by the Bears in the NFL as well as the Denver Broncos

Dick BUTKUS
CHICAGO BEARS ● LINEBACKER

Few players in NFL history have been as intimidating as the Maestro of Mayhem

of the rival American Football League, but he chose to stay near to his home-town of Chicago and became an instant fan-favourite at Wrigley Field. In his first game as a rookie, he recorded 11 unassisted tackles.

His predecessor at the MLB position, Hall of Famer Bill George, remarked: "The day he reported to training camp, I knew my days were numbered. There was no way he wasn't going to be great." Nicknamed the 'Maestro of Mayhem', Butkus had the speed and agility to make tackles from sideline to sideline and to cover running backs and tight ends on pass plays.

One Butkus quote, though tongue-in-cheek, summed him up: "I wouldn't ever set out to hurt anyone deliberately unless it was important – like a league game."

He simply defined the middle linebacker position; his instinctive hard-hitting play resulted in 22 career interceptions and he recovered 25 opponents' fumbles – an NFL record at the time of his retirement in 1973, when a serious knee injury cruelly ended his career.

THE MASTERFUL DIRECTOR

"Bradshaw had a rifle arm, size, intelligence and desire, and saved his best performances for the playoffs."

TERRY BRADSHAW

POSITION: Quarterback
NFL DRAFT: 1970/Round 1/Pick 1
CAREER: Pittsburgh Steelers (1970-1983)
• • • •
HIGHLIGHTS:
4 x Super Bowl champion (IX, X, XIII, XIV)
2 x Super Bowl MVP (XIII, XIV)
3 x Pro Bowl (1975, 1978, 1979)
Career TD-INT: 212-210
27,989 Career Passing Yards
2,257 Career Rushing Yards
23 Career Rushing TDs
Pro Football Hall of Fame (Enshrined 1989)

It took a bitter Terry Bradshaw almost two decades to forgive Pittsburgh Steelers fans after they jeered him off the Shea Stadium field on December 10, 1983. Having felt his elbow pop when tossing the second of two touchdown passes in a 34-7 win over the New York Jets, he exited in the second quarter. Already hurt by the team, who had not authorised his off-season elbow surgery nine months earlier, to Bradshaw this was the ultimate betrayal. After leading the Steelers to four titles, he thought he deserved better. Then followed personal demons, which included failed marriages and trouble with anxiety, a dicey acting career and a stint as a country singer.

Bradshaw had a rifle arm, size, intelligence and desire, and saved his best performances for the playoffs. But in the beginning of his 14-year career he struggled, often forcing his passes which resulted in interceptions.

He came out of Louisiana Tech with little knowledge of how to read defences or run a pro offense. Poor play, benchings and public squabbles with head coach Chuck Noll didn't endear Bradshaw to the Steel City, while his folksy Southern attitude was often misconstrued as a lack of smarts. Dallas linebacker Thomas Henderson told reporters before Super Bowl XIII that Bradshaw "couldn't spell 'cat' if you spotted him a 'c' and a 't'".

Once he matured as a signal-caller, Bradshaw led the Steelers to titles in January 1975 and 1976 as the masterful director of a run-oriented offense. By the time Pittsburgh won two more Super Bowls in 1979 and 1980, the offense revolved around his passing.

While his career ended in acrimony, he is now among Pittsburgh's favourite sons. Time heals wounds. Just a little longer is needed in some instances.

STEELERS

TERRY BRADSHAW • QB

Led the Steelers to four Super Bowl titles… **and was booed**

Despite leading the Steelers to four titles, Bradshaw was not always a fan favourite

Steelers

THE
LATE BLOOMER

"The biggest issue for me was playing professional football and showing up trying to be a regular law student"

STEVE YOUNG

POSITION: Quarterback
NFL DRAFT: 1984 Supplemental/Round 1
CAREER: Los Angeles Express (1984-85 USFL)
Tampa Bay Buccaneers (1985-1986)
San Francisco 49ers (1987-1999)

• • • •

HIGHLIGHTS:
3 x Super Bowl Champion
(XXIII, XXIV, XXIX)
Super Bowl MVP (XXIX)
7 x Pro Bowl (1992-1998)
2 x NFL Most Valuable Player (1992, 1994)
4 x NFL Passing Touchdowns Leader (1992-1994, 1998)
6 x NFL Passer Rating Leader
(1991-1994, 1996, 1997)
Career TD-INT: 232-107
33,124 Career Passing Yards
64.3 Career Completion %
4,239 Career Rushing Yards
34 Career Rushing Touchdowns
Pro Football Hall of Fame (2005)

T he last five quarterbacks to win the Super Bowl MVP award threw a total of 13 touchdown passes. Aaron Rogers threw three, Eli Manning one, Joe Flacco three, Tom Brady threw six in two games. Thirteen in five games. Steve Young threw six. In one game.

STEVE YOUNG

QB

Late bloomer Young went to seven consecutive Pro Bowls

GATE **D** | SECTION **122** | ROW **27** | SEAT **002**
LOWER LEVEL

SUPER BOWL XXIX

AFC-NFC World Championship Game
Sunday, January 29, 1995 · 6:00 P.M.
Joe Robbie Stadium, Miami
$200 All Taxes Included
Gates Open At 3:00 P.M.

Super Bowl XXIX
Sunday, January 29, 1995 · 6:00 P.M.
Joe Robbie Stadium, Miami
$200 All Taxes Included
L O W E R   L E V E L
GATE | SECTION | ROW | SEAT
D | **122** | **27** | **002**

Young's performance for the San Francisco 49ers against the San Diego Chargers in Super Bowl XXIX was one of the most superb by a quarterback in any game, never mind the biggest game. And the very next day he was in law school, having first decided to study in 1988, bored with backing up Joe Montana for four years. By the time he graduated, he had won the NFL MVP award twice and had been to the Super Bowl three times.

"The biggest issue for me was playing professional football and showing up trying to be a regular law student," said Young, who was rarely acknowledged as Joe Montana's equal, especially by Montana.

From the USFL to under-fire Tampa Bay Buccaneers starter to Joe Montana's backup to Super Bowl winner whose best years were in his mid-30s, Young took a unique road to the Pro Football Hall of Fame. He didn't start his 40th NFL game until 1992 – at age 31, in his eighth NFL season (and ninth in professional football).

In San Francisco, he benefitted from Bill Walsh's teaching, and not every QB gets to throw to Jerry Rice. Yet Young was a great quarterback, as he showed with his performance in the 49-26 shellacking of the Chargers, a team who had given up just 20 passing touchdowns all season. And he achieved that in little more than three quarters before coach George Seifert pulled him from the game. Heaven knows what he would have achieved had he had full game – and a full career as a starter.

THE GREATEST STEAL IN HISTORY

Seven Super Bowl rings and records galore – this is how a flabby sixth-rounder transformed into the most successful player in NFL history

TOM BRADY

POSITION: Quarterback
NFL DRAFT: 2000/Round 6/pick 199
CAREER: New England Patriots (2000-2019), Tampa Bay Buccaneers (2020-2022)
....
HIGHLIGHTS:
7x Super Bowl Champion (XXXVI, XXXVIII, XXXIX, XLIX, LI, LIII, LV)
5x Super Bowl MVP (XXXVI, XXXVIII, XLIX, LI, LV)
15x Pro Bowl (2001, 2004, 2005, 2007, 2009-2018, 2021)
3x NFL Most Valuable Player (2007, 2010, 2017)
NFL 2000s All-Decade Team
NFL 2010s All-Decade Team
5x Passing Touchdown Leader (2002, 2007, 2010, 2015, 2021)
Over 89,000 career passing yards
97.2 career passing rating

Nearly two decades ago, Tom Brady had the chance to spend the season asserting himself as the starting quarterback for the New England Patriots. He went from a little-known, unimpressive late draft pick to one of the NFL's very best players – perhaps one of the all-time greatest – but like almost every player in the league, he needed a little bit of luck to get him started.

Having been drafted the year before and thrown just three passes all year, he was given the chance to start when Drew Bledsoe, a three-time Pro Bowler at the time and franchise quarterback for eight years, suffered internal injuries in the second game of the season after a massive hit while playing against the New York Jets.

Brady led his New England Patriots to a remarkable victory in his very first Super Bowl

With the Pats 0-2 after an unspectacular start to the year, the 199th pick of the 2000 NFL Draft was thrown in to face the high-powered Indianapolis Colts. He had been comically slow at the Combine and plenty of teams passed over him before the Patriots picked him up. In his first full game, the 24-year-old threw for just 168 yards, albeit in a win, and a week later he would manage just 86 yards in a defeat to the Miami Dolphins. Few then would have expected him to lead the game-winning drive in the Super Bowl some months later, a performance that would define him for years to come.

The Pats had reached Super Bowl XXXVI thanks to 11 wins in Brady's 14 regular season games and playoff victories over Oakland, in overtime,

and Pittsburgh, on the road. In New Orleans, facing the St Louis Rams, New England appeared to have blown it when Ricky Proehl caught a 26-yard pass for a touchdown to complete a 14-point comeback and tie the game with only 90 seconds left on the clock. Fans steeled themselves for overtime in the biggest game of all for the first time ever.

But Brady had other ideas. Since that shaky start against the Colts and the Dolphins, he had secured 12 more wins as a QB and seemed to have the confidence of a far more experienced man. His numbers had been unspectacular when put in the context of the league – less than 3,000 passing yards and 18 touchdowns – but there were two crucial stats in play on this Louisiana evening: Brady had led four fourth-quarter comebacks and five game-winning drives.

Brady is one of only two players to have won five Super Bowls as a player

himself was not one for half-measures in the heat of the moment. "Go out there and sling it," the veteran quarterback on the sideline told the youngster who had usurped him.

If it had been a Hollywood movie, Brady might have thrown a massive bomb against all the odds to his wide receiver who would streak in for a game-winning touchdown. But this wasn't Hollywood and that wasn't Brady. Instead, he demonstrated the skills for which he has become famous across the NFL: grit, accuracy and an ice-cold nerve. If you were under any doubt as to how chilled out Brady was, even before the game started, consider that he popped his kit off 40 minutes before kick-off and had a nap in the locker room.

On the very first play of the drive, with pundits screaming for a zero-risk run play, Brady stepped back for the pass. Famous for not being a particularly outstanding athlete, he evaded three rushers in a collapsing pocket and got a short, simple pass off to running back JR Redmond. Getting up from the bottom of a 900lb pile, Brady banged his chest in celebration, a brief half-second he afforded himself before rushing up to the line of scrimmage.

Only Vinny Testaverde of the Jets, a veteran 13 years Brady's senior, could best the New England quarterback in both those aspects. And the Pats man had already done something similar that very evening, throwing his first Super Bowl touchdown to David Patten to complete a drive that had started with just 80 seconds left before half-time.

Perhaps any other quarterback, with no timeouts left, the two-minute warning gone and the scores tied, would have let the 1:21 left on the clock run out. "You have to play for overtime now," said the legendary John Madden on TV commentary duty. "You don't want to go for anything or do anything stupid."

But despite starting on his own 17-yard line, Brady wanted to go for it. Fortunately, he had a coach named Bill Belichick who agreed. He had backed Brady late in the draft, he had backed Brady when he was 5-5 as a starter and Bledsoe had returned healthy, and he was backing him now. Bledsoe

This time he scanned the sidelines where a receiver could get out of bounds and stop the clock, but the Rams defence were ready for that. And while a lesser man might have forced a square peg into a round hole, Brady knew he could still keep the game alive as long as he got some yardage. He hit Redmond in the middle of the field again and ran up to spike the ball. Next play, he looked around the whole field before throwing to Redmond again, who got out of bounds and stopped the clock. Now the Rams were on the run. They had been Super Bowl favourites all season. Now they were on the back foot against a second-year quarterback in his first full NFL season. They responded, flooding the pocket and forcing Brady to throw it away. But when Brady fired a strike to Troy Brown to get them into field goal range and Adam Vinatieri did the necessary to give the Pats the win with no time left on the clock, it completed one of the greatest finishes to a Super Bowl ever seen.

In less than two years, Brady had gone from a fourth-string quarterback who had been drafted in the sixth round, the seventh man in his position to come off the board, to Super Bowl MVP. One of the key figures behind his success was his head coach Belichick, whose star had risen at an almost identical time. A relentlessly hard-working and unapologetically irascible coach, he had worked for the New York Giants, the Cleveland Browns, the New York Jets and even for a short period the Patriots themselves as assistant under Bill Parcells, losing a Super Bowl to the Green Bay Packers. Four years later, Belichick returned to the top job.

Belichick's first season was a losing one. They finished 5-11 and owner Robert Kraft's decision to entrust almost every stage of the organisation's running to his new coach was starting to look like a poor one. In fact, that choice by Kraft linked Belichick's fate to Brady's forever, and the quarterback's success story is as much Bill's as it is Tom's.

Brady recalls after winning the Super Bowl MVP award in their first victory, he asked coach and mentor Belichick if he could break team protocol of flying home together to go and take part in the MVP's traditional trip to Disney World instead. Belichick's response was uncharacteristically carefree: "S***, yeah! How many times do you think you win the Super Bowl?"

Belichick was hardly to know that he and Brady would actually win the Super Bowl multiple times. After that first, remarkable win for Brady and the Patriots franchise, they added a second title two years later with a close 32-29 victory over the Carolina Panthers. The following year, The Patriots beat the Philadelphia Eagles to win their third Super Bowl in four years. A new dynasty was born.

But Brady always had a strained relationship with his head coach. Much of the time, the two worked well together. Both were hard workers, prepared to make sacrifices in their personal lives to be the best player and coach possible. But perhaps they were too similar, and as time went on, Brady and Belichick began to butt heads. The famously dour coach was hardly effusive in his praise of Brady.

LOOKING AFTER THE BALL
Brady has just a 1.8 per cent interception rate, bettered only by Aaron Rodgers among QBs with 70-plus games.

LASER ACCURACY
no player has completed more passes in the NFL than Brady

A COOL HEAD
Under pressure, there are few better quarterbacks in the league's history. Most use their feet to escape defenders: Brady uses his speed of thought.

STAYING INJURY FREE
Only 2008, when a double knee ligament tear ended his streak of 111 straight starts, saw Brady miss any notable time in his career return to the court after just eight months

PACE
Brady's 40-yard dash time at the 2000 NFL Scouting Combine was a slow 5.28 seconds. But he quickly defied the sneers

BRADY 12

TOM QB

"The biggest thing Tom does for us is to try to keep us out of those bad plays where we have 5 to 10 percent chance of really being successful, whether it's a coverage or a blitz or an alignment that they give us, and he sees that what we've got called just isn't what we want to be in," Belichick said, when asked to define what made Brady the player he is.

"That wasn't why we called the play, was to run it against that particular look. Then sometimes he'll be able to get out of those and get us something that, like I said, gives us more of a fair fight. That's a big job of the quarterback in our league, to not just manage the game in terms of getting the ball out of bounds and the clock and stuff like that, but also managing the game in terms of giving the offense the chance to run plays that are competitive because defences can get in certain alignments and really make it tough on you. Tom does a great job of that."

'Great job' barely covers it. As Brady aged, he seemed to get better. He and his team hit a purple patch in 2015, ten years after their third Super Bowl title. The Patriots secured their fourth with a nail-biting 28-24 win over the Seattle Seahawks. Brady was named Super Bowl MVP again, but he gifted his prize – a car – to defensive back Malcolm Butler, whose goal-line interception sealed the win. Two years later, Brady's New England Patriots mounted a special comeback from 28-3 down to the Atlanta Falcons to secure his fifth ring in 2017 – in overtime. And they followed that with another title two years later. If the team of the mid-2000s was a dynasty, the team of the mid-2010s was its successor. This time the Patriots won three Superbowls in five years – and Brady was still at the helm.

NOT TOTALLY PERFECT

Tom Brady was not without blemishes. The Deflategate scandal, where New England were found to have deliberately left less air in the footballs used for their offensive plays, saw his name dragged through the mud. Brady also invited controversy when one of Donald Trump's "Make America Great Again" caps was photographed in his locker. He vowed not to discuss politics after that – on the advice of his then-wife Gisele Bündchen. And critics complained that the Patriots' unbeaten regular season in 2007 did not end with Brady's hands on the Vince Lombardi Trophy due to the Giants' storied comeback in Super Bowl XXXXII. It was a testament to Brady's ability, however, that when he missed out on 2008 through injury, the same roster could only manage a record of 11-5. Rather than criticise Brady for not winning the Super Bowl in 2007, we should praise him for getting his team there.

Since that first unlikely Super Bowl win against the Rams, Brady has rarely entered big games as the underdog. His 27 postseason wins are unrivalled and his presence in the Hall of Fame at the first opportunity is assured beyond doubt. But he cannot be inducted into that elite club until he has been retired for five years. Brady finally hung up his helmet for good in 2022, having finally parted ways with Bill Belichick and New England in 2019. He spent his final three years in Tampa Bay, guiding the Buccaneers to the postseason every time and winning another Super Bowl ring.

That seventh and final title gave Brady a remarkable stat. He doesn't just hold more titles than any other player. He holds more than any other NFL team. And, by winning away from Coach Belichick, Brady proved beyond doubt that he really is the Greatest of All Time.

BRADY THROWS THREE TOUCHDOWNS IN COMEBACK WIN

969760647358

GATE	SECTION	ROW	SEAT
3	138	62	10
	SOUTH PLAZA		

SUPER BOWL
XLIX

SUNDAY · FEBRUARY 1, 2015 · 4:00 PM
UNIVERSITY OF PHOENIX STADIUM
ARIZONA
$500
Stadium Gates Open at Noon
All Taxes Included

SUPER BOWL XLIX
SOUTH PLAZA

GATE	SECTION	ROW	SEAT
3	138	62	10

Visit NFL.com/SBApp to download the Super Bowl GameDay App

Brady has become famous for his
cool head under pressure

THE GOLDEN ARM

> *"Hoping to make the most of the opportunity, 'Johnny U' saw his first pass as a pro intercepted. He never looked back"*

JOHNNY UNITAS

POSITION: Quarterback
NFL DRAFT: 1955/ROUND 9/PICK 102
CAREER: Pittsburgh Steelers (1955),
Baltimore Colts (1956-1972),
San Diego Chargers (1973)

••••

HIGHLIGHTS:
Super Bowl Champion (V)
3 x NFL Champion (1958, 1959, 1968)
10 x Pro Bowl
(1957-1964, 1966, 1967)
NFL Man of the Year (1970)
4 x NFL Passing Yards Leader (1957, 1959, 1960, 1963)
4 x NFL Passing Touchdowns Leader (1957-1960)
NFL 75th Anniversary All-Time Team
Career TD-INT: 290-253
40,239 Career Passing Yards
Career Completion %: 54.6
Pro Football Hall of Fame (Enshrined 1979)

Johnny Unitas was cut by the Pittsburgh Steelers before he even got a chance to throw one pass in a pre-season game. The ninth-round draft pick from Louisville then played semi-pro football with the Bloomsfield (Pennsylvania) Rams for $6 a game until Baltimore Colts' coach Weeb Ewbank decided to take a chance on the kid with the crew-cut. He signed him to a $7,000 contract.

Unitas got his second break when injury sidelined Colts starting quarterback George Shaw in the fourth game of the 1956 season. Hoping to make the most of the opportunity, 'Johnny U' saw his first pass as a pro intercepted. He never looked back.

Unitas, the NFL's three-time MVP, accumulated incredible stats during his 18-year career with the Colts and San Diego Chargers. When 'The Golden Arm' retired, he held virtually every meaningful passing record, including attempts (5,186), completions (2,830), yards (40,239), most 300-yard passing games (26), touchdown passes (290) and, incredibly, tossing a touchdown pass in 47 consecutive games.

But without a doubt, it is his heroic performance in the 1958 NFL title game, often referred to as the 'Greatest Game Ever Played', that he is best remembered. His tying and winning drives were examples of what it takes to win under pressure. Late in the game, with the Colts trailing the Giants 17-14, Unitas completed seven straight passes to set up a tying field goal with seven seconds left. He then executed an 80-yard touchdown drive in overtime to win the game. Unitas proved that sometimes all you need is a chance to play.

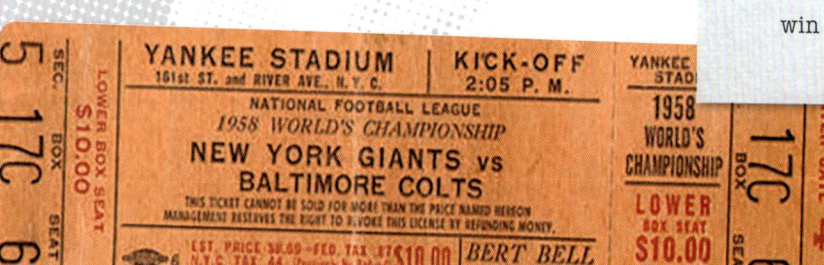

Johnny
UNITAS
BALT. COLTS • QUARTERBACK

'The Golden Arm' made the most of a second chance with Colts'

The 10-time Pro-Bowler was dubbed
'The Golden Arm' but was fortunate
to get a second chance in the game

THE
COMEBACK KID

In 1982, one play earned Joe Montana and the San Francisco 49ers a place in history, and heralded the beginning of one of the NFL's greatest dynasties

JOE MONTANA

POSITION: Quarterback
NFL DRAFT: 1979/Round 3/Pick 82
CAREER: San Francisco 49ers (1979-1992)
Kansas City Chiefs (1993-1994)
••••
HIGHLIGHTS:
4 x Super Bowl Champion
(XVI, XIX, XXIII, XXIV)
3 x Super Bowl MVP (XVI, XIX, XXIV)
8 x Pro Bowl (1981, 1983-1985, 1987, 1989-1990, 1993)
2 x NFL Most Valuable Player (1989, 1990)
NFL 1980s All-Decade Team
NFL 75th Anniversary All-Time team
Career TD-INT: 273-139
40,551 Career Passing Yards
92.3 Career Passer Rating
Pro Football Hall of Fame: (Enshrined 2000)

The playoffs of the National Football League's 1981 season seemed like any other: a mix of expected results, with some shocks and surprises thrown in. But they also marked a sea change; the genesis of a footballing dynasty that would go on to dominate the league in the decade to come. Standing in the way of this power shift was head coach Ray Perkins and his New York Giants, fresh from a battle with the Philadelphia Eagles at Veterans Park. Opposite them, the San Francisco 49ers and their cool-headed

Joe Montana in action for the San Francisco 49ers

hotshot quarterback, Joe Montana. Now in his third year of professional football, Montana, and the 49ers, were hungry for their first taste of Super Bowl glory.

The Giants had always been a strong contender in the NFC, playing a physical style of football on both offence and defence. The 49ers, on the other hand, were plucky and determined, but never consistent enough to be of any real threat. This time, though, something was different. At 25 years old, Montana had finally settled into his role, and with an offence gelled around him, his passing was consistently tearing defences to ribbons. The Giants were wary of a change, but they weren't expecting this.

"I don't think anyone saw it coming with them becoming the dominant team in the league for several years to come," recalls Perkins, now 70, in an interview with NewJersey.com. "They had some really great teams and played some really great football over the next four to five to six years. We certainly didn't see that coming, but that was the one game that got them over the hump."

A few months earlier, with the 1981 regular season looming, the 49ers had been readying themselves for another run at Super Bowl immortality. With his offence finally feeling complete around Montana, head coach Bill Walsh began building his defence into a fortress of muscle and steel. He revamped his secondary with rookies Ronnie Lott, Eric Wright and Carlton Williamson before giving experienced safety Dwight Hicks a more prominent role.

With these changes in place, the Niners had a slightly shaky start with losses to the Detroit Lions and Atlanta Falcons in the first three games of their campaign. Soon after, however, things began to shift rapidly into gear. Montana began throwing completed pass after completed pass, and Hicks and the rest of the defence started swallowing offensive plays like a black hole.

The team would go on to win all but one of their next 13 games, blowing their rivals away in a truly spectacular showing. The Niners' focus on the short passing game, and Montana's impeccable arm, helped them cruise through the regular season with a 13-3 record, winning the NFC West and also booking a place against the Giants at the 49ers' home, Candlestick Park.

In that game, the Niners threw everything at the Giants. Montana and company had become known as a team that came back from behind to win, but here, they went on from a 7-7 tie in the first quarter to totally dominate New York. By the second quarter, that lead was 17-10, which rolled into a 24-10 lead by half-time.

Montana was throwing short pass after short pass and wide receiver Dwight Clark was catching them like it was practice. The Niners refused to relent, and Montana pummelled the Giants defence until the final whistle was blown, calling time on a 38-24 win. Clark was easily Montana's favourite receiver with five passes for 104 yards and a touchdown. Next stop: the Dallas Cowboys. Next stop: The Catch.

That successful pass from Montana to Clark in the dying seconds of the NFC Championship Game on 10 January 1982 has become legendary among players, broadcasters, coaches and fans. When Clark leapt above defender Everson Walls, collecting the ball in the Dallas end zone for the winning touchdown, it created something electric: a moment in time that changed the fate of Montana and the rest of the 49ers forever.

Prior to that final drive, the game was a back-and-forth affair that Dallas was slowly winning in a war of attrition. It wasn't pretty, but it was getting the job done. Early on Montana had thrown a blinding 17-yard pass to Charle Young, and an even more impressive 24-yarder to Lenvil Elliott before an eight-yard pocket pass saw wide receiver Freddie Solomon trot over the line for a touchdown. Cowboys QB Danny White responded with a 20-yarder of his own before setting up a 44-yard field goal. And the Niners' hard-fought lead was soon erased when a fumble on the 29-yard line allowed White to throw for a 24-yard touchdown.

In the second quarter, things went from bad to worse when a Montana pass was intercepted in the end zone. But the ensuing Cowboys drive was eventually stopped, and it didn't take long for Montana to find his favourite pair of receiving hands, slotting a sweet 20-yard touchdown pass to Clark to make it 14-10. Dallas soon struck back. A five-yard rush over the line was all that was needed to retake the lead, following a controversial interception penalty that gave the Cowboys an extra 35 yards of scrimmage.

Montana seemed to lose his cool in the third quarter, a pass to running back Elliott bouncing out of his hands, but an interception by Niners linebacker Bobby Leopold spared his blushes. Montana then made an easy handoff to fleet-footed RB Johnny Davis to retake the lead at 21-17.

THE STEVE YOUNG QUARTERBACK CONTROVERSY

After more than a decade of leading the Niners offence, Montana sustained an elbow injury that put him out for the entirety of the 1991 season. The strain was so severe that Montana was forced to miss almost all of the next season as well, before coming on to play in the final game of the regular season against the Detroit Lions. Despite almost two years out, Montana proved he still had it, guiding the team to another win.

Second-string QB Steve Young had stepped into Montana's shoes in the interim, and had proved his worth, despite the Niners not making the playoffs in 1991. Young continued to start the following season, but many thought his days were numbered, as reports of a recovering Montana continued to surface. However, the deputy's growing confidence and performances ultimately won out. Montana would eventually be traded to the Chiefs.

"That pass in the dying seconds of the NFC Championship Game has become legendary"

The Catch has become arguably the most iconic moment in NFL history

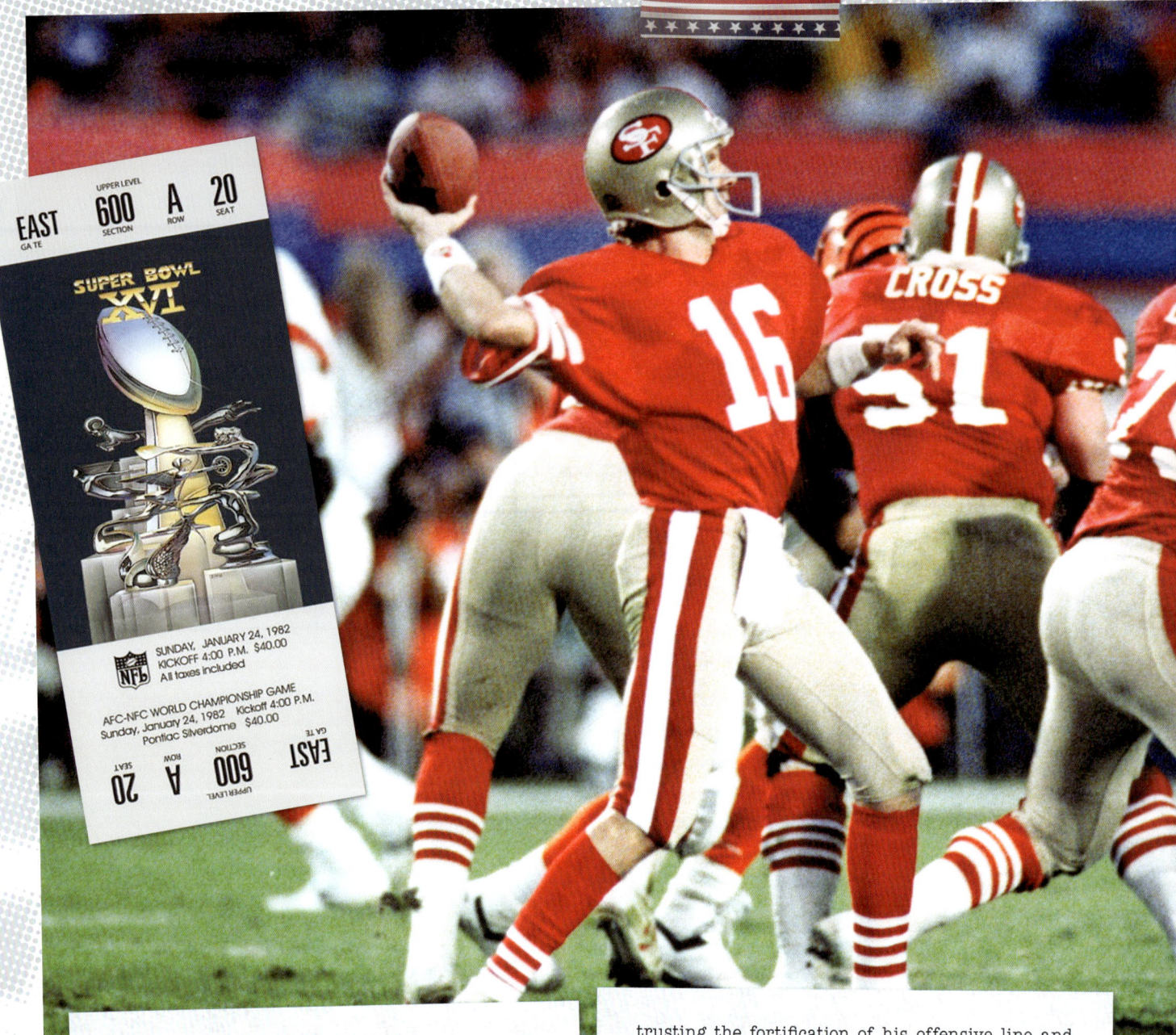

EAST
GATE
600
SECTION
A
ROW
20
SEAT
UPPER LEVEL

SUPER BOWL XVI

SUNDAY, JANUARY 24, 1982
KICKOFF 4:00 P.M. $40.00
All taxes included

AFC-NFC WORLD CHAMPIONSHIP GAME
Sunday, January 24, 1982   Kickoff 4:00 P.M.
Pontiac Silverdome $40.00

This clearly wasn't the Cowboys of old, their era of dominance was coming to a close, but it was still a team willing to grind through blood and sweat for a win. One minute into the fourth quarter and everything went wrong for Montana and the Niners. A 22-yard field goal reduced their lead, and then a fumble by RB Walt Easley set up White for a simple 21-yard touchdown pass to Doug Cosbie, storming the Cowboys into a 21-27 lead. With less than five minutes on the clock, Montana and his team had a lot of ground to cover.

Montana dug in, found his form, and embarked on an 83-yard drive that brought the Niners to the Cowboys' 6-yard line. The quarterback was keeping his cool,

trusting the fortification of his offensive line and scrambling away from any defenders fortunate enough to break through. No interceptions now. Just focused passing.

Next came 'the play', because behind every great catch, there's a play orchestrating the pieces. With 58 seconds left at third and three, Montana took the snap and prepared for a 'Sprint Right Option' that would have opened Freddie Solomon up for a pass. But Solomon slipped, leaving Montana without his intended target. A pass rush had also collapsed the offensive wall, with two defenders now bearing down on Montana. He didn't panic – he knew exactly where Clark would be, despite not being able to see the end zone. Sprinting towards the sideline, Montana

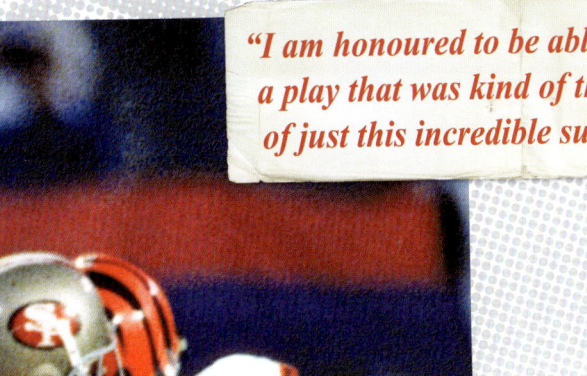

"I am honoured to be able to be a part of a play that was kind of the culmination of just this incredible surprise season"

threw an almost-desperate high pass over the onrushing defenders. The next thing he knew, the crowd was screaming. Touchdown. Kicker Ray Wersching made the extra point, and the 49ers were winning 28-27.

"It's humbling, really," commented Clark on making The Catch in America's Game: The Super Bowl Champions documentary. "I feel honoured people are still talking about it, 25 years later. I am honoured to be able to be a part of a play that was kind of the culmination of just this incredible surprise season. It's great to give 49er fans that moment that they can relive over and over and over, and I know they do because when I am in San Francisco and a lot of places, people want to talk about that play and how it crushed the Cowboys and sent them into submission for a decade."

For Montana and the 49ers, the win against the Cowboys – against 'America's Team' – in the NFC Championship Game was as important as their eventual victory over the Cincinnati Bengals in Super Bowl XVI. It was symbolic of a shift in NFL dominance, the mantle of power passing from one team to another. After years at the top of their game, the loss to Montana and the 49ers at Candlestick Park in 1982 signified the end of the Cowboys' time at the top. The guard had changed, and the Dallas Cowboys were out.

The win also heralded the beginning of the San Francisco 49ers as one of the true football dynasties of the 1980s. With Montana as their talismanic quarterback, the team began a run that would lead them to a total of four Super Bowl victories in the next nine years.

Montana changed the team, and some would say the entire league, forever with his focus on pocket passing, his never-say-die attitude, and his burning desire to win. Across his glittering career at the Niners, and later the Chiefs, Montana led his teams to 31 fourth-quarter come-from-behind wins. Few nicknames are as well-earned as 'The Comeback Kid'.

RETIREMENT PLAN: THE PRICE OF FOOTBALL

Joe Montana may have retired at the age of 38 in 1995, following 14 seasons at the San Francisco 49ers and two at the Kansas City Chiefs, but all those years of blood, glory and scrimmage took their toll – something Montana has been reflecting on ever since.

"The mental part was hard initially when I first retired," commented Montana to USA Today. "Because it's quick – cold turkey, the game's gone. Then the physical stuff tries to catch up with you."

Since his retirement, Montana has extreme pain in the muscles of his hands, a knee that won't straighten after four separate surgeries, and a neck that has needed three fuses and is headed for a fourth. As well as further surgery on his elbow, Montana also has nerve damage in one eye; the painful legacy of a career in the high-impact NFL.

TOTAL DOMINATION

An almighty combination of power and speed, Jim Brown's unparalleled talent shone brightly before Hollywood beckoned

JIM BROWN

POSITION: Fullback
NFL DRAFT: 1957/Round 1/Pick 6
CAREER: Cleveland Browns (1957-1965)
• • • •
HIGHLIGHTS:
NFL Champion (1964)
9 X Pro Bowl (1957-1965)
3 X NFL Most Valuable Player (1957, 1958, 1965)
8 X NFL Rushing Yards Leader
(1957-1961, 1963-1965)
NFL 75th Anniversary All-Time Team
NFL 1960s All-Decade Team

Jim Brown is a curiosity in that he is considered one of the greatest football players ever – if not the all-time number one – despite the fact that only a fraction of living NFL fans witnessed his career.

Lining up at fullback – at the time the primary ball-carrying position – he played each of his nine NFL seasons with the Cleveland Browns, leading the team to the NFL championship in 1964. Brown was invited to the Pro Bowl in every season he played, picked as a first-team All-Pro in all but one. He also led the NFL in rushing yards in eight of those seasons, and was named the Associated Press' league MVP three times – including in 1957, his rookie season. Jim Brown was a serious ball player.

But the other notable thing about Brown, the son of a professional boxer and a homemaker, is that he retired at the peak of his powers, at the age of 29, to pursue a career as a movie star and social activist. Announcing his retirement in the UK, in a press conference on the set of The Dirty Dozen, in which he starred, he stated that he had simply achieved everything he had wanted to. "I never looked back," he later said.

As Chinese philosopher Lao Tzu said, the flame that burns twice as bright also burns half as long. The move was, in part, motivated by the fact that his film was running behind schedule. He was also seeking a 'more mentally stimulating' vocation, and had already begun formally working within the African American civil rights movement.

Brown's early departure from pro football prompts the question of what greatness is. Is it measured by championship rings? If so, excellence in this sport is summed up by the methodical and sustained accumulation of titles, as Joe Montana did, and Tom Brady continues to do. Or is it defined by those players who provide rare but memorable moments of brilliance like Brett Favre? What about those, like Brown, who change the sport itself through their utter domination of both their position and their league, albeit briefly?

Certainly, Brown – who would be described as a running back today – played his position like no other. Highlight reel footage makes it look like he was playing against teenagers. A man of exceptional physical gifts, he was both as quick as lightning and able to run over defenders. It frequently took three or four opposition players to take him down. Some of his runs simply defy belief. Footage exists of Brown

JIM BROWN
RUNNING BACK   CLEVELAND BROWNS

Jim Brown played each of his nine NFL seasons with the Cleveland Browns, winning three league MVP awards

shrugging off three defenders and dragging his feet from boggy playing fields, before reversing the field and racing past the chasing pack. Viewed in the context of the era in which he played, it makes the mind boggle.

Given the physical advances made in professional sports – and in pro football especially – it says a great deal that the Jim Brown of the mid-1960s looked as if he could have played in the NFL of 2020. Or as Peter King, the widely-respected NFL writer, told the New York Daily Post: "He dominated more than any quarterback has, and he did it in a time when the running game was everything. He was as big as a linebacker, as fast as a receiver. Imagine averaging a 100-yard game for your career. He averaged 104.3."

Lawrence Taylor, the New York Giants' Hall of Fame linebacker and longtime friend of Brown's, put it more bluntly, describing him as a "beast, built like a brick s**thouse".

Brown averaged a mammoth 5.2 yards per carry across his 118 career games in pro football – a stat none of the sport's other greats at the position can match. Walter Payton averaged 88 yards per game to Brown's 104.3, and 4.4 yards per carry, while Emmitt Smith racked up 81.2 yards each game and 4.2 yards per carry. His 1963 season, in which he averaged 133 yards per game, has only ever been bettered by O.J. Simpson's 1973 season. Brown's six career games in which he scored four TDs remains an NFL record; LaDainian Tomlinson and Marshall Faulk each have five.

As he departed the league, Brown left as the record-holder for single-season and career rushing yards – 1,863 and 12,312, respectively – and was the all-time leader in rushing touchdowns, total touchdowns and all-purpose yards. As the man himself put it: "When running backs get in a room together, they don't argue about who is the best."

While most of Brown's records have since been broken, it is important to bear in mind that NFL rushers now play 16 regular season games a year; Brown played 12 in his first four seasons and 14 in his final five. The icing on the cake of Brown's career undoubtedly came in the 1964 NFL championship game, the Browns' triumph over the Baltimore Colts in Cleveland Stadium. The highly-rated Colts were led by Don Shula, who was named NFL Coach of the Year in only his second season, and one of the league's best quarterbacks in Johnny Unitas.

The game itself was played in hostile conditions; at kick-off the wind whipping across the stadium from Lake Erie reached up to 30 miles per hour. The first half was scoreless, as both offenses struggled. Despite all eyes focusing on Brown – not least those of the Colts defenders – he had a quiet day by his standards. A turgid game ended 27-0 in the Browns' favour.

But it mattered not; this was unequivocally Jim Brown's team. He had dragged them to the title game with a string of superhuman performances, and his shadow still looms large over Cleveland. The Browns haven't won a title since, and the city would only taste sporting triumph again 52 years later, when LeBron James' Cavaliers won the 2016 NBA championship. The team would reach the NFL championship game the following year, but were blown out 65-12 by Vince Lombardi's Green Bay Packers at Lambeau Field. Lombardi, the master tactician, devised a scheme to neutralise Brown, assigning middle linebacker Ray Nitschke to mark Cleveland's star player all day. Also stressing the importance of ball control, Lombardi restricted his opponents to just 38 offensive plays. Brown's last-ever professional game, it was a sad end to what may be the greatest NFL career of all time. He officially announced his retirement six months later as the call of Hollywood proved too strong.

Dick LeBeau, the Detroit Lions' Pro Bowl defensive back who would later find fame as the defensive mastermind behind two of the Pittsburgh Steelers'

Super Bowls, said: "Jim Brown was a combination of speed and power like nobody who has ever played the game. You just didn't know if you were going to get a big collision or be grabbing at his shoelaces."

A physical and intellectual giant of Brown's size may never be seen again by the league, on which the fullback's legacy is clearly imprinted. Having gone from a respected civil rights champion to an unlikely supporter of President Donald Trump, Brown's political influence has most definitely waned of late. But what remains, thankfully, is the memory of a true NFL great.

But the most surprising thing may have been Brown's self-perception. Unlike the watching world, he maintained he was no special talent, instead putting his success down to sheer force of will, saying he 'never laid out' in any of his 118 pro games. "I played nine seasons and I never missed a game," he said. "I might not have the greatest ability of everybody, but the one thing that stands is that when it was time to play, I was there."

Jim Brown was picked sixth overall by the Browns in 1957 after playing college football at Syracuse University

AMERICAN ALL-STAR

An All-Star in both baseball and football and a college track-and-field superstar... is Bo Jackson the greatest athlete in history?

BO JACKSON

POSITION: Running Back
NFL DRAFT: 1986/Round 1/Pick 1
CAREER: Los Angeles Raiders (1987-1990)

••••

HIGHLIGHTS:
Pro Bowl (1990)
5.4 Career Yards Per Carry

Ask anyone to name the greatest sportsperson the world has ever seen and you'll get a range of answers: Pelé, Muhammad Ali, Steffi Graf, Usain Bolt. Names known the world over.

But there's one name that should undoubtedly make the list; one that sports fans outside of the US may not have heard. For those that know the name Bo Jackson, however, it's easy to see why people describe the man from Alabama as the greatest athlete in sports history.

From an early age, Bo was talented on the track, in baseball and in football, and by the end of his career he was the first player in history to be made an All-Star in the two major sports. One story that is often overlooked thanks to Jackson's astonishing achievements though, is how he almost decided to forego his football career entirely.

Jackson had an overall batting average of .250 at the end of his career, hitting 141 home runs

It was a dramatic time for Jackson, who had been playing, and excelling, in both baseball and football since his early high-school days. After winning the Heisman Trophy during his senior year for his exceptional performance in college football, the Tampa Bay Buccaneers drafted Jackson, and the team's management invited him to visit, flying him out to Florida on owner Hugh Culverhouse's private jet. The team reportedly assured Jackson that officials had checked with the National Collegiate Athletics Association (NCAA) and that the trip, which could have cost him his collegiate eligibility, had been approved. Jackson was also told that, if he chose to sign for the Bucs, he would be required to quit baseball entirely and be a one-sport athlete – a tough decision for a young man of such exceptional talent.

When Jackson returned to Auburn University, however, he was duly informed by his baseball coach that the trip had not been approved, and that the NCAA considered it to be a violation of the rules. Jackson was immediately ruled ineligible to play the remainder of the baseball season, and despite the Bucs' best efforts to help him appeal, the bridge was burned.

Jackson has since spoken about the situation, explaining that he thinks the Bucs tried to force him to drop his baseball career in favour of signing for their team – that if they declared him ineligible for baseball, he would be forced to focus on football. He was convinced that, because he was having such an impressive senior season in baseball, the NFL team

thought he would give up his football career to focus on the other sport, and that their actions were a desperate attempt to stop him from doing so.

Jackson was understandably furious that Culverhouse had lied to him, and vowed that if the Buccaneers drafted him he would refuse to sign. He made good on his promise later that year, and so they forfeited his rights before the end of the 1987 draft.

Fortunately, Jackson's career in sport was not over by any means. In 1986, despite the fact that he had been ruled out of the game for half a season, Jackson was drafted by an MLB team, the Kansas City Royals. He signed for them and, after spending a year playing for the Memphis Chicks (the Royals' Class AA minor league affiliate) he made the Royals roster in 1987.

Finally able to show what he could do on the field on a major stage, and burned by his experience with the Bucs, Jackson seemed committed to being a one-sport athlete. But before the 1987 NFL draft ended, Bo was drafted again – this time by the Los Angeles Raiders.
Curious, he met with the owner of the Raiders, Al Davis, and they came to an agreement that would allow Jackson to continue to play baseball as well as playing in the NFL. A contract was negotiated where Jackson would be permitted to see out the entire baseball season with the Royals before reporting to the Raiders for the remainder of the football season. Not only that, Davis also offered Jackson an extremely generous salary.

For Bo, this was the perfect scenario – not only did he get to continue with his baseball career, he could also test his ability on the football field in the pro sphere. In his first season with the Royals, Jackson hit 22 home runs with 53 runs batted in and ten stolen bases as a left-fielder. Not a bad start for his first season in the majors, but it was in the 1989 season that he really started to showcase his talents.

That year Jackson was voted to start for the American League All-Stars – a team made up of the best players in the league. The team then faced off against their National League counterparts, and after catching a line-drive to save two field runs, Jackson hit a monstrous 137-metre home run to open his side's first inning. At the conclusion of the game he was unanimously named MVP for his stellar play on both offense and defense.

CAREER OPTIONS

As if going pro in two major US sports wasn't enough, in school Jackson had another option that he could've pursued – track and field. He competed in decathlon, and was a two-time state champion in the competition. Both times, he built up such a commanding points lead before the final event (the 1500m) that he never even competed in the race, and still won the gold medal. He also set state school records in high jump and the long jump.

Despite his pro career being cut short by injury, Jackson still became the first player to be named an All-Star in two sports

JACKSON 34

Of course, throughout these years, he was also playing the majority of games for the Raiders in the NFL. In 1989, the same year that he was named an All-Star for the Royals, he also had his most prolific season as a football player. In the 11 games in which he played, Jackson rushed for 950 yards and scored four touchdowns as the team's feature running back. The next year he rushed for 698 yards and scored five touchdowns over the ten games he played to earn Pro Bowl honours – making him the first player in history to be named to All-Star teams in two major US sports. He was at the very top of both his games.

However, in January 1991, disaster struck. Jackson was on the receiving end of a seemingly routine tackle at the end of a 34-yard run during a Raiders playoff game, which resulted in a career-ending hip injury. Despite surgery in

1992, Jackson was never able to return to the football field – it was the premature end of the star's NFL career.

But injury didn't totally end his sporting life. Jackson made a triumphant return to the baseball diamond in 1991, where he played two seasons with the Chicago White Sox, appearing in 108 games in total. According to an interview with ESPN, Jackson promised his mother that once he recovered from hip surgery, he would hit a home run for her. Sadly, before he could make his return, she passed away. In his very first inning after surgery, Jackson hit a home run to right field. He reportedly had the ball encased and bolted to the dresser in her room. In 1994, after just seven years as a professional, he retired once and for all – his status as an all-time great secure.

THE GUNSLINGER

An all-action star who was pure box office – both on and off the field

From the improvised scrambles to the throws that broke receivers' fingers in practise, the tobacco-chewing gunslinger had a turbo-charged right arm and a killer football brain.

The only player to be named MVP for three straight seasons (1995-97), Brett Favre waltzed into the Hall of Fame after transforming the fortunes of a proud, but ailing, franchise.

Before his trade to Green Bay from the Atlanta Falcons in 1992, the Packers had made the playoffs just twice in 24 years. With Favre, they made the postseason 11 times in 15 years. They reached the Super Bowl in consecutive seasons, winning the first in 1997.

An iron man with a heart of a lion, Favre made 297 consecutive starts, or 321 including playoffs. Favre even suited up the day after his father's sudden death, giving the performance of his career in Oakland in December, 2003.

His annual flirtation with retirement became a running joke but in the 2007 season, his last in Green Bay, Favre took the Packers to an overtime loss to the New York Giants in the NFC Championship Game.

Favre left Lambeau Field under a cloud and spent a season with the New York Jets before joining the Minnesota Vikings in 2009. He still hasn't been forgiven in the deepest parts of Wisconsin.

The first of his two seasons in purple was magical, propelling the Vikings to 12-4 with over 4,000 yards. With 19 seconds to go and in field goal range, a battered Favre threw an interception in the NFC Championship game and the New Orleans Saints won in overtime. Vintage Favre. He finally retired after an injury-hit 2010 with records, and fans, galore.

BRETT FAVRE

POSITION: Quarterback
NFL DRAFT: 1991/Round 2/Pick 33
CAREER: Atlanta Falcons (1991)
Green Bay Packers (1992-2007)
New York Jets (2008)
Minnesota Vikings (2009-10)
····
HIGHLIGHTS:
Super Bowl Champion (XXXI)
11 x Pro Bowl (1992, 1993, 1995-1997, 2001-2003, 2007-2009)
3 x NFL Most Valuable Player (1995-1997)
71,838 Career Passing Yards
297 Consecutive Games Started (321 including playoffs)
First Player To Beat All 32 NFL franchises
Pro Football Hall of Fame (Inducted 2016)

Brett Favre of the Green Bay Packers walk off the field after a game against the Minnesota Vikings

THE KING OF MIAMI

Dan Marino was the Dolphins' unstoppable pass master – a gifted quarterback who surgically tore defences apart

DAN MARINO

POSITION: Quarterback
NFL DRAFT: 1983/First/27
CAREER: Miami Dolphins (1983-1999)

••••

HIGHLIGHTS:
9 x Pro Bowl
(1983-1987, 1991, 1992, 1994, 1995)
NFL Most Valuable Player (1984)
61,361 Career Passing Yards (5th All-Time)
420 Career Touchdowns
(5th All-Time)
13 X 3,000-Yard Seasons
(2nd All-Time)
First Player To Pass For 5,000 Yards In a Single Season
Pro Football Hall of Fame (Enshrined 2005)

DAN MARINO   QB

W as Dan Marino the greatest quarterback not to win a Super Bowl? Almost certainly. But was he the NFL's greatest-ever quarterback?

If you were building a prototype signal-caller, Marino had all the attributes: tall, calm under pressure, mentally and physically strong with a lightning-fast release and laser-like right arm. In terms of pure pocket passing, there is no-one better.

A fierce competitor, Marino transformed the fortunes of the Miami Dolphins, despite playing alongside a 1,000-yard rusher just once in his 17 seasons. That was in part due to Miami's preponderantly passing offense, but that Marino propelled the Dolphins to the postseason ten times is all the more remarkable as he could only lean on a top-10 defense for four seasons during that spell.

A natural leader, Marino inspired those around him, coaxing performances out of a sometimes less than stellar supporting cast. He began throwing to the 'Marks Brothers' – Clayton and Duper – and while both were serial Pro Bowlers, Irving Fryar was the only other Pro Bowl receiver on Miami's roster during

Marino was idolised by the Dolphins fanbase during his 17-year career in Miami

the Marino era. On the durability front, few were as reliable. Marino played 145 straight games, a record which ended in 1993 after he tore his right Achilles tendon in Cleveland. But in true Marino style, he bounced back, winning Comeback Player of the Year in 1994, after throwing for 4,453 yards and 30 touchdowns.

Marino's mantra was a simple one: "There is no defense against the perfect pass. I can throw the perfect pass." He built his reputation at the University of Pittsburgh, and won the Rose Bowl months before the draft, but his stock plummeted due to mysterious – and unfounded – rumours of drug use. Five quarterbacks, among them fellow future Hall of Famers Jim Kelly and John Elway, were taken before the delighted Dolphins plundered Marino with the 27th overall pick.

The husky youngster immediately began to make an impression with his aura and ability impressing Hall of Fame coach Don Shula. The pairing between Shula and Marino should not be underestimated.

''From the moment he walked in, everything you saw about him, you liked. He's just a down-to-earth guy from Pittsburgh, blue-collar people, warm people," Shula told the New York Times in 1984. "I've compared this guy to Larry Csonka in personality. He's always around the locker room like 'Zonk' was in our Super Bowl years, he just enjoys being around the other players."

After a promising training camp, it took Marino six games to supplant David Woodley as starter and he began to swat records aside as he did pass rushers during his golden career. His rookie season was a sign of things to come, the confident Marino guiding Miami to 12-4 and the AFC East, throwing 20 touchdowns on his way to the first of nine Pro Bowl selections.

Marino entered his second season aged 22 and went on to compile one of the finest campaigns in NFL history, once again ripping up the quarterback record books. MVP Marino propelled the Dolphins to a place in the Super Bowl, becoming the first

"Marino was the only quarterback capable of outwitting and outplaying the ferocious '85 Chicago Bears"

Marino was just 22 when he began to rewrite the record books with his unforgettable 1984 season

quarterback to top the 5,000-yard barrier – his 5,084 yards were 470 more than his nearest competitor. Leading the Dolphins to 14-2, Marino threw for a then NFL-record 48 touchdowns, 16 more than the nearest competitor. In the AFC Championship game, Steel City native Marino passed for a record 421 yards and threw four touchdowns against the Pittsburgh Steelers to seal his first – and only – trip to the Super Bowl with a 45-28 win. It remains the highest-scoring AFC Championship game.

And so to Stanford, where the depleted Dolphins faced one of the greatest teams of all time. In what was practically a home game for the 49ers, Joe Montana outdueled Marino, who completed 29 of 50 passes for 318 yards, passed for one touchdown and threw two interceptions. But while the 49ers were a team with a rigid defense, solid special teams and a fully functioning offense, Marino couldn't do it on his own. A suspect offensive line saw him sacked four times, while the Dolphins would only run the ball nine times,

such was the unpredictability of the running game.

The 38-16 defeat was rough on Marino, who swore he would return to the game's biggest stage. "I want to know what it's like to play in a Super Bowl and win one. My career will be great without it. But, personally, selfishly, I want to know what it feels like," Marino said. It is a sporting tragedy that the game's greatest prize eluded Marino, but it should not detract from his place in the pantheon of NFL greats.

"What he accomplished was to have a better season than anyone who has ever played this game," fellow Hall of Fame quarterback Roger Staubach said. "I'm talking about quarterbacks, wide receivers or anyone else. He was unbelievable." While Marino's compelling CV is missing the game's biggest prize, he was the only quarterback capable of outwitting and outplaying the ferocious '85 Chicago Bears.

After breaking and tossing aside quarterbacks at will,

head coach Mike Ditka had steered the Bears to 12-0 as they stomped into Miami for an eagerly-awaited Monday night game on December 22, 1985. Defensive co-ordinator Buddy Ryan and his fabled 46 defense hadn't conceded a touchdown in 13 quarters and Chicago had outscored its previous three opponents 104-3.

Four games away from becoming the second team to go unbeaten in the regular season, members of Miami's 1972 undefeated team were in the stands. No pressure then. While Chicago had much to play for, Miami did too. On the back of a three-game winning streak, the Dolphins needed a win to keep the New England Patriots and the New York Jets at bay in the race for a wide open AFC East. Against relentless blitzes, Marino's quick release, speed of thought and laser-like arm exploited one-on-one mismatches, surgically picking Chicago apart.

In their previous six games, Chicago had allowed a total of 29 points. By half-time, the Dolphins had put 31 on the board. Ditka and Ryan were at each others' throats over the use – or lack thereof – of a nickel cornerback to counter Miami's spread offense and use of Nat Moore as an extra receiver. Marino finished the game 14-for-27 for 270 yards with three touchdowns and an interception, with the win moving the Dolphins to 9-4. They won out, claiming the AFC East title and storming into the AFC Championship game, but the Patriots intervened to prevent a rematch with the Super Bowl-winning Bears. Again, Marino had been thwarted.

He reached the AFC Championship game once more, losing to the Buffalo Bills in 1993, but that was as close as he would get to the Vince Lombardi Trophy. Marino continued to amass passing records, toppling Hall of Famer Fran Tarkenton as career passing leader in attempts, completions, yards and touchdowns in 1995.

Shula was replaced by Jimmy Johnson in 1996 and a change in mentality saw Miami re-establish the run game, making the Dolphins less reliant on Marino for his final four seasons. His final game, a 62-7 defeat to the Jacksonville Jaguars in the 1999 playoffs, was no way for such a fine player to sign out, but such is sport sometimes.

Inducted into the Hall of Fame in 2005, Marino finished his career with 61,361 yards, 420 touchdown passes, 252 interceptions, and a quarterback rating of 86.4. Yes, he didn't win a Super Bowl, but his staggering career totals revolutionised the NFL. Not only that, defenses knew he was going to pass – they just couldn't stop him.

THE FAKE SPIKE

Dan Marino made 420 scoring passes, but there is little doubt which is the most memorable. Facing the New York Jets (6-5) in late November, 1994, the Dolphins (7-6) were on a two-game losing streak and trailing 24-6 late in the third quarter.

But Marino hit a purple patch and the largest crowd in Jets history was silenced by one of the great gadget plays ever witness in the NFL. Fourth down on the Jets eight-yard line with 22 seconds remaining. Marino bellows: "Clock! Clock! Clock!" and gestures a spike with his right hand. "He still has one timeout. He'll save that for the field goal," says NBC analyst Paul Maguire.

But Dolphins receiver Mark Ingram knew exactly what was going through Marino's mind. The Jets didn't. Only three defenders moved, one of them rookie cornerback Aaron Glenn who had his back to the play. It was too late, Ingram darting to the right of the end zone to reel his fourth touchdown of the half, capping a 28-24 victory. Pandemonium ensued.

The Jets didn't recover for several years, their season sent into a tailspin with popular head coach Pete Carroll sacked in the offseason. But the play breathed life into the Dolphins' season, winning the AFC East in Don Shula's penultimate year as head coach.

THE MINISTER OF DEFENSE

FLEER '96

GREATEST GAME
4 SACKS AGAINST MINNESOTA
9/26/88

Reggie White

DEFENSIVE END

Truly great players elevate not only themselves, but those around them. Reggie White didn't just play well – he made his whole team play well

REGGIE WHITE

POSITION: Defensive End
NFL DRAFT: 1984 Supplemental/Round 1/Pick 4
CAREER: Memphis Showboats (1984-1985)
Philadelphia Eagles (1985-1992)
Green Bay Packers (1993-1998)
Carolina Panther (2000)

••••

HIGHLIGHTS:
Super Bowl Champion (XXXI)
13 x Pro Bowl (1986-1998)
2 x Defensive Player of the Year (1987, 1998)
2 x NFL Sacks Leader (1987, 1988)
NFL 1980s All-Decade Team
NFL 1990s all-Decade Team
NFL 75th Anniversary All-Time Team
198 Career Sacks (2nd All-Time)
Pro Football Hall of Fame (Enshrined 2006)

It's quite difficult to make the position of defensive end sexy. The majority of men standing, or crouching in a three-point stance, are well over six feet tall and upwards of 300lb. They are not twinkle-toed side-steppers whose fancy skills are going to make it onto many highlight reels.

But anyone watching the game tape of Super Bowl XXXI could hardly avoid the impact of one Reggie White.

White had made his name in Philadelphia, but after his contract expired, he was a free agent. Green Bay Packers coach Mike Holmgren had failed to make the playoffs in his first season in the football-mad corner of Wisconsin and realised that he could save himself the time spent planning for White by signing him.

But Holmgren knew he would have to pull out all the stops to get his man, given his reputation in the NFL as one of the best defenders in the game. Knowing White to be a devout Christian and an ordained Baptist minister, Holmgren took a gamble. He called the player up and left a message on his answer phone: "This is God. I want you to play in Green Bay."

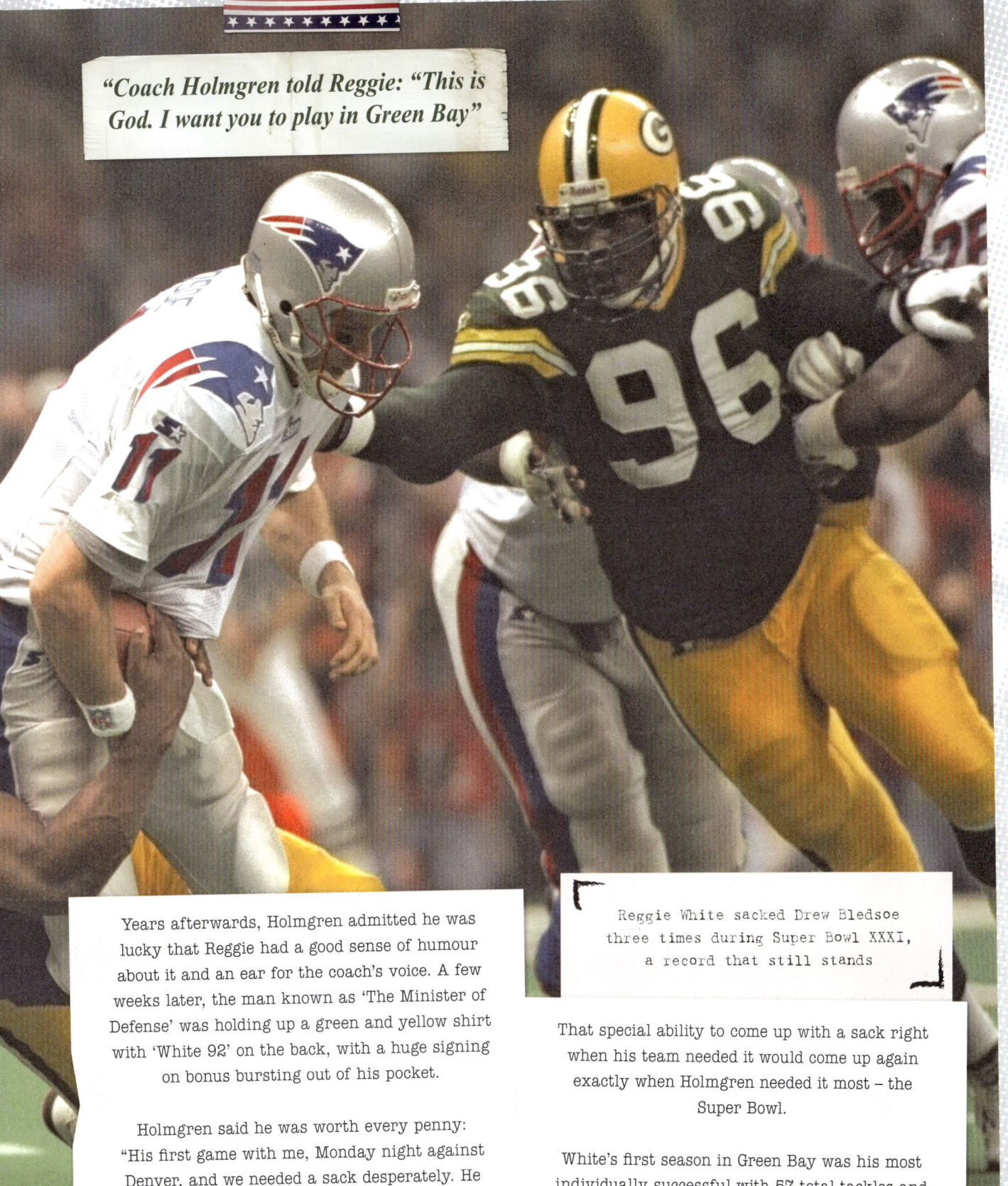

> *"Coach Holmgren told Reggie: "This is God. I want you to play in Green Bay"*

Years afterwards, Holmgren admitted he was lucky that Reggie had a good sense of humour about it and an ear for the coach's voice. A few weeks later, the man known as 'The Minister of Defense' was holding up a green and yellow shirt with 'White 92' on the back, with a huge signing on bonus bursting out of his pocket.

Holmgren said he was worth every penny: "His first game with me, Monday night against Denver, and we needed a sack desperately. He sacked John Elway twice in a row right at the end of the game to allow us to win the game. He was special."

Reggie White sacked Drew Bledsoe three times during Super Bowl XXXI, a record that still stands

That special ability to come up with a sack right when his team needed it would come up again exactly when Holmgren needed it most – the Super Bowl.

White's first season in Green Bay was his most individually successful with 57 total tackles and 13 sacks, but it was not until 1997 – his fourth year with the franchise – that he would take them to the very top.

Reggie White was always a well-liked but also feared defensive back

White led the NFL in sacks in back-to-back years when he was at the Philadelphia Eagles

In the regular season, he led the team with 8.5 sacks but the figure itself was not of his usual high standards. It was one of just three occasions he had failed to reach double figures in the regular season, and that included an ill-advised return from retirement with Carolina in 2000.

In the playoffs too, he was without a sack. It was perhaps because at this point, teams knew at least one thing about the Packers defense: stay away from Reggie White. But just as he had on that Monday night against Denver, Reggie came good eventually.

The New England Patriots had ground their way to the Super Bowl, led by quarterback Drew Bledsoe and backed up by a defense that conceded just nine points in their two playoff games. They had scored 48 too and had plenty of offensive weapons, but few gave them a chance of beating Reggie White's Green Bay Packers.

Holmgren had bred a lean, meaning winning machine. For White's lack of explosive, statistical form, Green Bay had conceded fewer points than any other team, with the defensive line's suffocating pressure creating easy opportunities for turnovers – they plundered five in the divisional playoff game against the 49ers. It is a mark of their abilities that

quarterback Brett Favre threw for just 79 yards in that game – but his Packers still scored 35 points. The Panthers in the NFC Championship game were similarly strangled.

It meant Green Bay were overwhelming favourites – 14 points with the Vegas oddsmakers – for the Super Bowl against a Patriots team the media said lacked substance. But they showed there was more to them than that, coming back from a 10-0 deficit to lead football's biggest game at the end of the first quarter.

They fell behind again but another touchdown, courtesy of running back Curtis Martin, narrowed the gap to seven points and while Desmond Howard's 99-yard kick-off return restored the two-score lead with 18 minutes of game clock left, Green Bay did not believe they were home and hosed. Bledsoe was finding his men with alarming regularity and White had yet to get to the quarterback.

And just as they needed 92 to step up, he did in the most spectacular fashion.

Lined up against right tackle Max Lane, a stalwart of the 1990s Patriots offensive line, White faked to the outside before cutting back to his right and charging straight through the blocker to reach Bledsoe within seconds of the ball being snapped. The quarterback picked himself up off the Astroturf shaken but still ready to lead a game-saving drive, albeit with a few more yards to make up.

Then White did it again.

Lane, desperate not to get beaten on the same side again, forced White to the outside, where he used his speed and power to run around the block he had just barrelled through to record consecutive sacks. Going to ground was all Bledsoe could do to stop White stripping the ball out of his hand. At 4th & 19, the Patriots were forced to punt the ball away and Green Bay's defensive leader had well and truly come to the party.

And 15 minutes later, White all-but wrapped things up his way. Inside the last two minutes and trailing by 14 points, Bledsoe dropped back in hope rather than expectation of finding an open man. White found himself up against Lane again and put him on his back with a casual one-armed swat, before grabbing the knees of the quarterback and securing his Super Bowl-record third sack of the game. The images of him sprinting to the end zone afterwards and holding the trophy up to the heavens will live long in the memory.

His professional football career had been given something of a false start by the summer-season USFL, which lasted just three years. White played there for two years before being signed by the Philadelphia Eagles as something of an unknown quantity. But that didn't last long.

He made 52 sacks in his first three seasons in the league and earned the NFL Defensive Player of the Year award by reaching the quarterback 21 times in just 12 games in 1987. He made himself a legend in Philadelphia and in 2008 was voted their greatest ever player in an ESPN fan poll.

But one of White's defining qualities, according to those who coached him, was not just his own ability. Once he had established himself as a defensive monolith, opposing offensive coordinators started to help out their forlorn right tackles and across the rest of the line, gaps opened up. Ultimately a team player, White was just happy to be winning games.

He should now be revered as one of football's greatest players, although his Sundays would likely be spent in church rather than at his beloved football field. He learned Hebrew after retiring and went to Israel on a pilgrimage.

But at the age of just 43, the cardiac and pulmonary sarcoidosis White had lived with for some years tragically took its toll.

THE UNITED STATES FOOTBALL LEAGUE

Since the NFL-AFL merger in 1970, American football had existed in relative stability, without threat or competition.

But Louisiana businessman David Dixon had spied a gap in the market, a yawning summer break in which no football was played for months on end. In the 21st century, this is filled by 24-hour news networks and endless speculation, but Dixon wanted to fill it with football.

And so he did. Having conceived the idea in the mid-60s, it did not come to fruition until its inaugural season in 1983, when three divisions of four teams played 18 games each between March and July. The Michigan Panthers won the first ever championship at Mile High Stadium in Denver, live on ABC across the country. Even Donald Trump wanted in, buying the New Jersey Generals.

A year later, University of Tennessee star Reggie White was given the chance to play professional football in the state where he had become a hero and could not resist signing for the Memphis Showboats.

Even though the 'Boats were far from world-beaters – they won 18 and lost 18 in his two seasons there – White established himself as one of the country's best pass-rushers before the league collapsed in 1986.

THE LEGEND OF ELWAY

After falling at the final hurdle three times, John Elway seemed destined to miss out on Super Bowl glory. But the Broncos' icon had other ideas...

JOHN ELWAY

POSITION: Quarterback
NFL DRAFT: 1983/Round 1/Pick 1
CAREER: Denver Broncos (1983-1998)

••••

HIGHLIGHTS:
2 x Super Bowl Champion (XXXII, XXXIII)
Super Bowl MVP (XXXIII)
9 x Pro Bowl (1986, 1987, 1989, 1991, 1993, 1994, 1996-1998)
NFL Most Valuable Player (1987)
NFL 1990s All-Decade Team
51,475 Career Passing Yards
(6th All-Time)
Pro Football Hall of Fame (Enshrined 2004)

For many fans the most memorable play ever made by John Elway, one of the greatest passers in NFL history, was a third down run in Super Bowl XXXII. In a desperate attempt to make a first down, with the scores tied in the third quarter, he threw himself headfirst into a crowd of defenders with enough force to send his 37-year-old body spinning 180 degrees in mid-air, before crashing to the turf with a thud.

The play, known as the Helicopter play, was the perfect visual metaphor for Elway's moment of redemption. After three painful Super Bowl losses in his prime, the talented wunderkind had become the grizzled old pro who'd do anything to win a football game.

Plenty of all-time great NFL quarterbacks enjoy less-than-stellar college careers, but that wasn't Elway's story. Not John Elway. Blessed with the build of a shortstop, the blonde-haired West Coast kid looked the part before he'd even been drafted.

It was as clear as day that he had it in him to reach the sport's pinnacle. The problem was that a number of major league baseball franchises felt the same way.

The 1983 draft, which also boasted future Hall of Famers Dan Marino and Jim Kelly, as well as Tony Eason and Ken O'Brien, has since become known as the greatest quarterback draft class of all time. Elway was picked first, by the Baltimore Colts. But, unimpressed with the dreary Colts franchise, he refused to sign, threatening to join the New York

Yankees instead. A disgusted Terry Bradshaw, who had won four Super Bowls with the Pittsburgh Steelers, said at the time that Elway should choose baseball because 'he's not the kind of guy you win championships with'.

How different the NFL of the 1980s and 1990s would have been had he followed Bradshaw's advice. Instead Elway managed to get a trade to the Denver Broncos. He had a mixed beginning to life in the NFL. While he led his team to a 13-3 record in 1984, and then an 11-5 season a year later, he failed to win a single playoff game in any of his first three seasons. The young signal caller did, however, show a glimpse of one his biggest attributes – his clutchness.

JOHN ELWAY

7

Topps

BRONCOS QB

Inducted into the Denver Broncos' Ring of Fame in 1999, Elway is the only player for whom the customary five-year wait has been waived

Elway prepares to throw the ball downfield during a game in 1987, his MVP year, against the Los Angeles Raiders

Only Tom Brady (7) can better John Elway's record of five Super Bowl appearances

ELWAY THE BASEBALL STAR

John Elway, one of the most talented all-round athletes in NFL history, was a much-coveted prospect coming out of college – and not just for his quarterback play.

In the 1981 draft, the New York Yankees used the final pick of the second round to snap up the Californian golden boy. He was given a $140,000 bonus – more than the draft's number one pick, Mike Moore. Future Hall of Famer Tony Gwynn, who enjoyed a distinguished career with the San Diego Padres between 1982 and 2001, was taken six picks later.

Elway played just one season in the minor leagues, with Class A Oneonta in '82, hitting for a sterling .318 average with four home runs in 151 at-bats.

It was no gimmick; the future Hall of Fame quarterback was a bona-fide baseball player and could easily have pursued a professional career had he so wished. He was one of a long line of athletes who have been drafted by both NFL and Major League Baseball franchises, which includes Bo Jackson, Deion Sanders and Russell Wilson.

Some commentators have judged Elway's foray into baseball to be part of his attempt to leverage a trade from the Baltimore Colts to Denver. In the end, it would appear his decision to stick with football was the right one.

In the penultimate week of the 1983 season, the rookie QB found himself 19-0 down to the Baltimore Colts. Staring down the ultimate humiliation – a loss to the team he had spurned – Elway managed to pull out something special. Hitting his receivers for three scores in ten fourth-quarter minutes, he stunned the Colts, nabbing their playoff spot to boot. Although his team crashed out of the '83 playoffs, losing to the Seattle Seahawks in the AFC wild card game, there was hope.

In the end, numbers can only tell so much of a story. One of the reasons Elway is remembered so fondly is that his 16-year career was sprinkled with some truly heart-stopping moments. Watching a quarterback drive the length of the field to make a decisive score is one of the greatest pleasures the sport has to offer. Elway's nerveless ability to grab victory from the jaws of defeat was as much one of the hallmarks of the NFL in the 1980s as his team's famously garish 'Orange Crush' jerseys.

The most famous of these, known simply as 'The Drive', came in the AFC Championship of the 1986 season.

Trailing the Cleveland Browns 20-13 with five minutes on the clock, Elway began on his own two-yard line, staring at 98 long yards of grass separating him from the Browns' end zone. Broncos guard Keith Bishop reportedly turned to his teammates, telling the huddle: "We've got them right where we want them." A short completion to running back Sammy Winder, followed by a short run, put Denver in a bind at third down on their own ten-yard line. Timeout.

Winder ground out three tough yards to move the chains, to a collective sigh of relief from Denver fans. They were still alive. No longer backed up against his own end zone, Elway started playing with more freedom. An 11-yard QB run was followed by passes for 22 and 12 yards. But just as quickly as the Broncos had gained the momentum, the door was slammed in their face. An incompletion and an eight-yard sack had Denver at third-and-18 inside Cleveland's half at the two-minute warning.

But with unerring calmness Elway hit rookie wide receiver Mark Jackson for 20 yards. Two more big plays – a pass and another quarterback scramble – ate up big chunks of yardage. On Cleveland's five-yard line, Elway then connected with Jackson once more – this time in the end zone – to tie the game up. The game was won with a 33-yard field goal in overtime.

In the current era, which has been dominated by cold-blooded performers like Tom Brady and Aaron Rodgers, it's easy to forget how rare it was to see quarterbacks maintain such sangfroid in the clutch. It would be another two years before Joe Montana's 92-yard game-winning drive in front of John Candy to win Super Bowl XXIII.

The high of the Cleveland game would be followed by a painful 39-20 loss to the New York Giants in Super Bowl XXI. It was the first of three Super Bowl losses in a four-year stretch for Elway and his men. The defeats to the Washington Redskins and San Francisco 49ers were by wide margins. But Elway would not be deterred, with the quarterback's moment in the sun coming at the conclusion to the 1997 season.

Tight playoff wins over the Kansas City Chiefs and Pittsburgh Steelers led the Broncos to the Super Bowl in San Diego's Qualcomm Stadium. It was a true fairy tale, but few expected them to beat the reigning champion Green Bay Packers, who boasted the league's best player in Brett Favre and an 11-point favourite tag. With the game tied at 17-17 on third down in the third quarter, Elway's famous 'Helicopter play' might have been the difference on the day. It was just enough to move the sticks, and the resulting touchdown put Denver in control.

The elder statesman of quarterbacks getting thrown around like a rag doll was painful for all concerned – not least those who had to watch. But John the Californian golden boy was now Elway the gamer. He rose to his feet with a primal scream. A fourth-quarter touchdown run by the Terrell Davis, the game's MVP, clinched it, but it was Elway who had finally scaled the mountain. After three Super Bowl losses, his career would have been horribly blighted had he not won one. He followed it up the next year with another Super Bowl win against the Atlanta Falcons, also taking the game's MVP award. It was his last game in pro football.

But if those rings weren't enough, Elway is also credited as the architect of Denver's Super Bowl 50 win, convincing Peyton Manning to join the Broncos over the 49ers and Tennessee Titans for one last Super Bowl push. Now the Broncos' general manager, Elway told Peyton he knew exactly what it felt like to yearn for a ring with the clock ticking on his professional career.

Neither man did it the easy way, but they got there in the end.

Elway looks on during a preseason game against the Detroit Lions

In his second career, Elway holds the Lombardi trophy as Denver's general manager after Super Bowl 50

WELCOME TO PRIMETIME

In 1989, the NFL was moving away from its sporting tradition and becoming a global phenomenon. Few players characterised this more than Deion Sanders

DEION SANDERS

POSITION: Cornerback
NFL DRAFT: 1989/Round 1/Pick 5
CAREER: Atlanta Falcons (1989-1993)
San Francisco 49ers (1994)
Dallas Cowboys (1995-1999)
Washington Redskins (2000)
Baltimore Ravens (2004-2005)
••••
HIGHLIGHTS:
2 x Super Bowl Champion (XIXX, XXX)
8 x Pro Bowl
(1991-1994, 1996-1999)
NFL Defensive Player of the Year (1994)
NFL 1990s All-Decade Team
19 Career Defensive Touchdowns (2nd All-Time)
Pro Football Hall of Fame (Enshrined 2011)

SCORE 1989 ★ ROOKIE

DEION SANDERS
CORNERBACK

Right from the beginning of his career in the National Football League with the Atlanta Falcons, Deion Sanders has kept people talking. Arguably the finest cornerback to ever play the sport, Sanders was a personality that made the NFL more accessible to everyone. His 'Primetime' moniker was well suited to a time when the game was moving away from its roots, and people would often tune in just to see the Florida-born defensemen who was fast becoming a star.

Appearances can be iconic, and Sanders' was just that. With the idea of an NFL Sunday just beginning to come to fruition, where matches were spread across the entire afternoon and evening for television coverage, he would often be pictured warming up in a languid fashion, with his signature bandana comfortably in place. These shots were never before of interest, yet the public loved him.

But sporting characters are only appreciated if they are talented and nobody could suggest the Florida State collegiate star wasn't fantastically gifted. What made Sanders memorable was the fact he was different. He was unique and he made the game of football appear both fun and easy in equal measure. However, what truly made his reputation stand the test of time was his production on the field.

At one time or another Deion Sanders dominated all the great receivers of his era, even Jerry Rice regularly struggled against the agile defender. Sanders was supremely athletic and his play benefitted from this. He could afford to take risks with his positional play, allowing a receiver to believe he had a yard or so advantage, before conjuring up a play out of nowhere. Wideout after wideout saw throws that seemed destined for them snatched away at the last.

Over the course of his career he recorded 53 total interceptions, a figure that would have been much higher had it not been for opposing offenses simply avoiding throwing to his side of the field. If you take a quick stock check of the best cornerbacks in the 2017 NFL, every single one has taken something from the former Dallas Cowboys defender. This is his sporting legacy; people have taken what he brought to the game and utilised for their own success.

Many younger viewers will hold Richard Sherman's cornerback play within the Seattle Seahawks infamous 'Legion of Boom' in the highest regard. His game-winning interception in the NFC Championship game against the San Francisco 49ers in 2013 was followed by a spectacular on-camera rant about wide receiver Michael Crabtree and how Sherman was the self proclaimed 'best corner in the game.'

A Super Bowl winner with both the 49ers and the Cowboys, Sanders brought success with him wherever he played

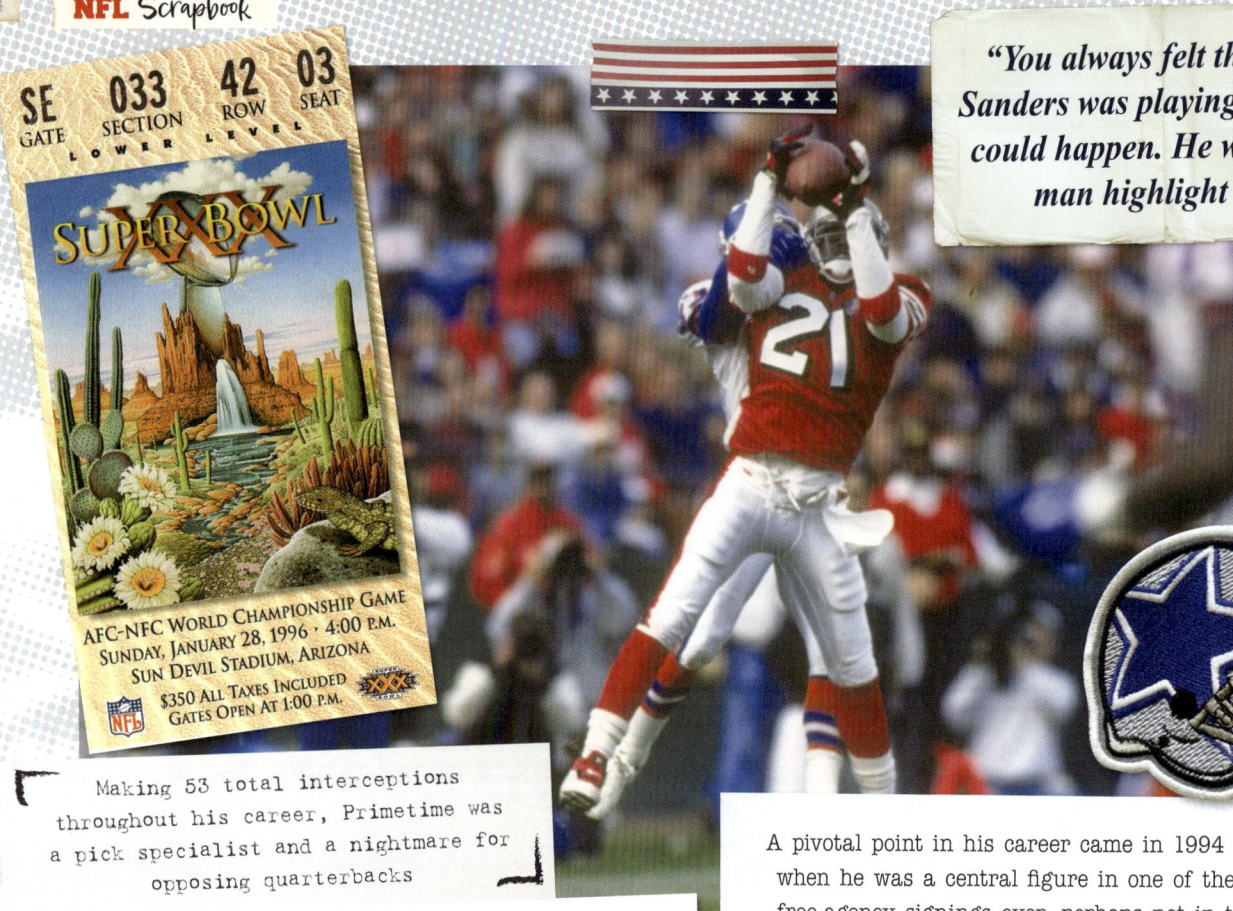

SE GATE **033** SECTION **42** ROW **03** SEAT
LOWER LEVEL

SUPER BOWL XXX

AFC–NFC WORLD CHAMPIONSHIP GAME
SUNDAY, JANUARY 28, 1996 · 4:00 P.M.
SUN DEVIL STADIUM, ARIZONA

$350 ALL TAXES INCLUDED
GATES OPEN AT 1:00 P.M.

"You always felt that when Sanders was playing, anything could happen. He was a one-man highlight reel"

Making 53 total interceptions throughout his career, Primetime was a pick specialist and a nightmare for opposing quarterbacks

This confidence, this penchant for the dramatic was classic Deion Sanders. This box-office environment, where defensive players had such a voice, was cultivated by Sanders back in the 1990s.

You always felt that when Sanders was playing, anything could happen. He was a one-man highlight reel; he remains one of just two players in football history to have scored a touchdown in every possible way. Occasionally he would line up on offense as a receiver, this experience both helped his individual stock as a player and directly influenced his catching skills at the cornerback position.

A common theme among the greats is how their natural talent is supplemented by an incredible work ethic. Deion Sanders was a meticulous film room regular. He would study plays in his own free time and even take an early portable DVD player with game highlights on longer flights, something that wasn't yet the norm when he was drafted. His insight into the game helped him too; he didn't just study opposing players, but opposing offensive coordinators too. He could spot patterns in the play-callers who had been in the league for a while and was of the thinking they would be in their positions for years to come. He was gaining knowledge he could reuse over and over.

A pivotal point in his career came in 1994 when he was a central figure in one of the biggest free-agency signings ever, perhaps not in terms of salary but in how newsworthy it was at the time, and how successful it ended up being. After five seasons in Atlanta, Sanders' sheer determination to win a championship saw him sign to play a single season with the San Francisco 49ers.

The league's top corner was joining one of its true powerhouse teams. Under George Seifert as Head Coach and with Steve Young as the team's starting quarterback, the Niners had everything necessary for Super Bowl success. Yet two successive conference championship defeats to the triplet-inspired Dallas Cowboys had left a sour taste in the mouth of those in the Bay Area. The solution? Go and sign Deion Sanders to a whopping $1.2 million contract.

Sanders adored the spotlight and he always performed accordingly. So respected was he by the San Francisco locker room, that several of the team's established stars agreed to take pay cuts to their own annual salary, simply in order to ensure this deal got over the line. The 49ers now finally had the shutdown corner to take on Dallas' Michael Irvin and Alvin Harper. With the spotlight on Sanders, the 1994 season proved to be his best in the league; he made six interceptions, starred in the victory over the Cowboys in the NFC Championship game and then duly won his first Super Bowl.

Off the field, Sanders recorded and released an album and hosted Saturday Night Live, but that was Deion, he could wear multiple hats, or rather bandanas, and nothing would slip. His performances on the field remained consistently high and he now had the Super Bowl championship that his play warranted. Not only did Primetime assist the modernisation of the sport as a whole, he helped revolutionise his own position on the field. Defenders will never be the true stars of the league – quarterbacks will always hold that distinction – yet Sanders made it possible that a cornerback could be viewed as an elite difference maker.

His ability to close off an entire side of the field made for a shift in defensive strategy. In the 1990s when passers like Joe Montana, Dan Marino and the aforementioned Steve Young dominated the league, many defensive coordinators were too afraid to utilise man-to-man coverage.

In teams with Sanders in the position, it was the exact opposite. So dominant was he in one-on-one matchups, his defensive coordinators simply abandoned the policy of zone defense and allowed him to do his thing up against a receiver.

There are even two separate 'Deion Sanders Rules' named after him, the first of which came when he participated in the 1989 Sugar Bowl, despite the fact he hadn't attended any classes that semester at Florida State University. Local education officials soon made it law that participation in bowl games couldn't come without completion of classes.

The second relates to his 1995 free agency deal with Jerry Jones' Cowboys. As a way to circumvent the salary cap he was offered a minimal base salary with a signing bonus of near $13 million. The league then mandated that a proportion of every signing bonus would count against the cap. Everyone was always talking about Deion.

Inducted into the Hall of Fame as a first-ballot candidate in 2011, Neon Deion's sporting legacy is enshrined in Canton; his achievements will remain for all to see. It is easy to remember Deion Sanders the world class cornerback, yet the complete package is what made him such a gift to the NFL. As he once put it himself, he got people to watch the sport and come to games when they previously wouldn't. "They don't pay nobody to be humble. Some people will come out to see me do well, some will come out to see me get run over, but love me or hate me, they're going to come out."

His 14-year career, albeit with a short retirement in that time, will go down as one of the greatest of all time, and rightly so. Primetime was a joy to watch. The way he played the game has paved the way for so many others; a Hall of Fame spot is richly deserved for one of the true NFL legends.

THE TWO-SPORT STAR

Whilst difficult to imagine now given how all-encompassing the NFL is throughout the year, Deion Sanders was actually a two-sport star at a professional level. Alongside his career in football, he also enjoyed a successful run in Major League Baseball, even making a World Series appearance with the Atlanta Braves in 1992.

His popularity combined two audiences and both sports benefitted. Fans of the cornerback would tune in to watch him as a center fielder and vice versa. He was a box-office attraction and his natural athleticism meant it wasn't merely a publicity stunt. He was an outstanding performer in both sports. What is even more amazing is that he took part in both sports concurrently. Sanders would play football on Sundays, and during the MLB playoff season take part in baseball matches during the week. He remains the only ever sportsman to both score a touchdown and hit a major league home run in the same week.

In a nine-year career that saw him turn out for the New York Yankees, Atlanta Braves, Cincinnati Reds and the San Francisco Giants, Sanders played 641 total games with 558 hits and 39 home runs. His athleticism helped him steal 186 bases. Mixing two sports isn't something totally radical, but performing at such a high level in both, professionally, certainly was. Primetime simply took it in his stride, his mission was to perform any way and in any environment he could, and perform is exactly what he did throughout his two-sport career.

Deion Sanders registered eight hits off 15 at-bats in the 1992 World Series

THE PASS MASTER

What makes Peyton Manning one of the best of all time? Anyone who played with him has a plethora of answers...

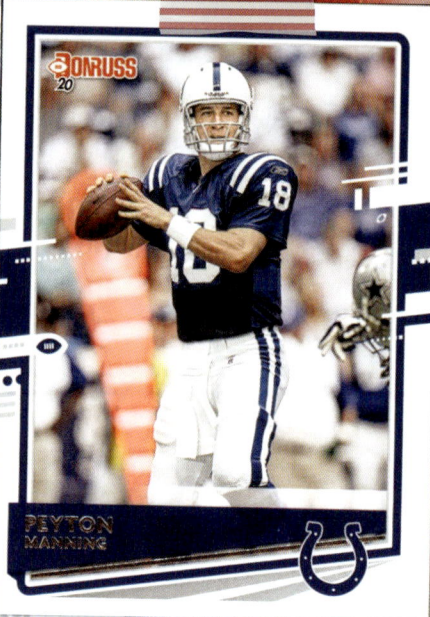

PEYTON MANNING

POSITION: Quarterback
NFL DRAFT: 1998/Round 1/Pick 1
CAREER: Indianapolis Colts (1998-2011)
Denver Broncos (2012-2015)

••••

HIGHLIGHTS:
2 x Super Bowl Champion (XLI, 50)
14 x Pro Bowl (1999, 2000, 2002-2010, 2012-2014)
5 x NFL Most Valuable Player (2003, 2004, 2008, 2009, 2013)
NFL 2000s All-Decade Team
Most Passing Yards in a Single Season (5,477 in 2013)
Most Passing Touchdowns in a Single Season (55 in 2013)
71,940 Career Passing Yards
(1st All-Time)
539 Career Passing Touchdowns (1st All-Time)

The balls are just so accurate - it's like a long hand-off sometimes." "He lives, eats, breathes, smokes, snorts, chews football. He's just a machine." "He's at the PhD. level. He's able to preview information in the huddle ahead of time."

All of these men have played with Peyton Manning and all of them have tried to explain why the New Orleans-born quarterback will go down as one of the greatest of all time. None of them have come up with the same answer – which should tell you that there probably isn't one. He is as close to the complete quarterback as anyone in the modern game of American football has come.

Perhaps the greatest compliment paid to Manning in fact came in one of his darkest moments. Having been given the franchise tag in 2011 by the Indianapolis Colts, a team he spent a total of 13 years with, Manning signed a new five-year deal worth around $90 million just a few weeks before undergoing another neck surgery on a long-standing injury. The operation was not expected to keep him out for any of the following season.

However, during pre-season training and rehabilitation, he complained of being unable to complete his faithful throwing action and had lost arm strength. It was his weapon, his strength and his everything. Without his arm, he was nothing. Doctors told him he needed a second operation that would rule him out for the entirety of the 2011 season.

Heart-broken, he was sent a message by Tom Brady, his career-long rival and contemporary. The two are always pitted against one another in the 'greatest' arguments that are held ad infinitum on bar stools across America and the world.

"To me, he's the greatest of all time," Brady said.

"If you don't draft me, I promise I'll come back and kick your ass"

Peyton Manning appeared at the Pro Bowl 14 times in his career, a joint NFL record

"He's a friend of mine, and someone that I always watch and admire, because he always wants to improve, he always wants to get better, and he doesn't settle for anything less than the best.

"So, when you watch the best and you're able to learn from the best, hopefully that helps me get better."

But Brady's words, however remarkable or comforting, could not fix the truth. Manning was facing a season watching 38-year-old Kerry Collins run the Colts' offense from the sidelines. He had already spent an agonising summer training in secret in Denver, unable to use the Indianapolis facilities due to an NFL-wide labour lockout. He had started out working with an old college friend in an underground

batting cage. The first pass he threw went five yards.

But his efforts to relearn throwing the ball were in vain, and that second surgery left him disconsolate. But he also, even after a decade, says he learned something about himself: "that I could persevere."

He had to. Manning was turned loose by the Colts in March 2012 before they would have to pay him a $28m bonus, and with the chance to draft Andrew Luck first overall beckoning. Manning, then 35, could not hold back his emotion at his final press conference with the team.

"Thank you for letting me be your quarterback," he told Colts fans, who had watched the team nose-dive to a 2-14 season without him. It was not something they had grown used to in the preceding seasons under Manning's influence.

Before he was drafted in 1998, there had been whispers on the inside of the NFL about a lack of arm strength, limited mobility and that taking him first overall in the draft would be a mistake. Washington State's Ryan Leaf had far greater potential to be a generation-defining franchise quarterback. Scouts around the league quietly informed a narrative which Sports Illustrated records as it being "fashionable to depict Manning as the safe pick, with Leaf cast as the potential mother lode". But it was telling that none of those insiders criticising Manning would go on the record, perhaps fearing that their words of warning would be quoted back at them for years to come if wrong.

But a week before the pick was announced, the Colts' new general manager Bill Polian still hadn't made up his mind. The pressure was well and truly on for the man who had taken the Carolina Panthers to within one win of the Super Bowl in only their second season of existence. The Colts had won just three games in that previous year and Polian, charged with making things right again, had a tough choice between Leaf and Manning.

Manning decided to up the ante.

"If you take me, I promise you we will win a championship," he told Polian in private.

"If you don't, I promise I'll come back and kick your ass."

They took him, but after a year, Polian was probably

OMAHA! MASTERING THE AUDIBLE

Manning approached the line of scrimmage with a play already picked out by the coach, every element of it planned out in advance to allow him to scan the field and pick the perfect pass.

But that was far from where the play-planning ended and in Manning's case, that was where the magic started.

The quarterback became famous for his ability to scan a defense and pick gaps before the ball had been snapped, calling audibles at the line to manoeuvre his team into a dangerous position to exploit them.

The cry of "Omaha, Omaha" followed by a series of words and numbers became a familiar one for Indianapolis – and NFL – fans, and more often than not it would be followed by the announcer's call of "Touchdown Colts!".

But the mystery over what exactly Manning meant by his "Omaha" shouts grew with his legend, until finally he agreed to answer the question at a press conference.

"Omaha is a run play, but it could be a pass play or a play-action pass, depending on a couple things: the wind, which way we're going, the quarter, and the jerseys that we're wearing."

That's right. Some things we'll never really know, and that makes it even more intriguing.

wondering if he could put enough of the right people around Manning to deliver those rings he had promised. The 3-13 record of 1997 was repeated in 1998 as the defense shipped nearly 30 points a game – but Manning remained a bright spark. He broke five different rookie records, including most touchdown passes in a season (26) and most games with more than 300 passing yards (four) – he only failed to find the end-zone on one game all year.

The league was ripe for a changing of the guard at quarterback. Some have called 1998 the 'last hurrah' of the great generation of signal-callers that arrived in the 1980s: Vinny Testaverde, Randall Cunningham, Steve Young, Dan Marino and John Elway were all well into their 30s while Troy Aikman was 32. Manning looked ready to take over.

And take over he did. From 28 picks and 13 losses in 1998, he ended 1999 with just 15 picks and 13 regular season wins, leading the Colts to an AFC East title, the No 2 seed and a first-ever playoff game in Indianapolis. He also passed 4,000 yards for the first time, something he would do in every single one of his full seasons after the first, a testament to his consistency and dependability.

Manning lost a close game to Tennessee in the 1999 playoffs but there was plenty to be optimistic about going forward. The 13 wins of that season represented a high watermark for Manning's first seven years at the franchise, even if little of that was down to his own performance.

The move from the AFC East to the AFC South in 2002 should have made things easier and back-to-back 12-4 seasons secured Manning consecutive division titles and league MVP awards – but still he could not propel them to the playoffs. In both of those seasons, he was eliminated by his great rival Brady, and the questions about his physicality were raised again.

Both those playoff defeats came at Gillette Stadium in Massachusetts and both times in freezing temperatures. The arm strength problems scouts had quietly identified in college were down to a congenital weakness in his neck, discovered by doctors after Peyton's oldest brother Cooper quit football as a teenager with spinal stenosis. Even though the younger Manning's neck problems would come later in his career, this apparent inability to cope with the cold and its effects on his throwing arm were a major worry.

So it was a further testament to Manning's abilities when he, having lost six straight times to Brady including those two play-off games beat the Pats two years in a row, and both at Gillette. The second win came in the 2006 season with Manning in red-hot form, despite the sub-zero conditions. After back-to-back 300-yard games, the Colts QB proved he could do it whatever the weather to take his team to 8-0 for the season. Despite sliding to 12-4, Manning hardly looked back that year. After two MVP titles without a ring, he was determined to deliver on that promise to Polian all those years ago.

And when he met the Patriots again in the AFC Championship game, it was down at the RCA Dome, Manning's first post-season clash with the Patriots on home turf in a match-up later billed by NFL's Greatest Games as 'Peyton's Revenge'. It was an all-out thriller as

Manning was often criticised for his lack of mobility but still enjoyed massive success in the NFL

"Thank you Colts fans, for letting me be your quarterback"

THE MANNING FAMILY ARE ALL CHAMPIONS

Christmas in the Manning household is probably littered with stories of sporting success. Peyton and Eli have split four Super Bowls and father Archie was an NFL draft second overall pick.

The oldest Manning brother Cooper might also have made it, as a promising basketball and football prospect, had he not been diagnosed with spinal stenosis as a teenager.

the Colts trailed 21-6 at half-time and even 28-18 going into the fourth quarter. In that second half, Manning marshalled three separate touchdown-scoring drives of over 75 yards, with Joseph Addai's three-yard run with just a minute left giving the home side the decisive four-point lead that would send Manning to his first Super Bowl. After such a remarkable, cathartic and spectacular win, fate seemed to finally be on Manning's side. The Colts were seven-point favourites to overcome the Chicago Bears and did so 29-18 to win Manning, who only threw one touchdown in the game, his first Super Bowl ring.

He would take the season MVP two more times with the Colts, adding three more divisional titles to his trophy cabinet, but he would never reach those heady heights again. He came close in 2009, losing out to New Orleans in Super Bowl 44, which saw him play the role of villain against the heroic post-Hurricane Katrina Saints.

But it was not over for Manning. After finding himself a contract with the Denver Broncos in 2012, Manning settled into the state where he had first discovered the full extent of his neck injury. And there he proved that the more things change, the more they stay the same. He led them to Super Bowl 48, where the Seattle Seahawks blew them out 43-8. He recorded double-figure winning seasons in each of his first four years. And then in 2015, he finally did it again at Super Bowl 50.

But for once, Peyton wasn't the star of the show. Denver had made it to the playoffs on the back of the league's top defense while Manning had thrown just nine touchdowns in the nine games he started. Injury reared its ugly head once again and he missed nearly half the regular season. But when the playoffs came around again, Manning once again came good. He booked a place in the Super Bowl 50 with another post-season win over Brady, throwing two touchdowns and crucially no interceptions in a 20-18 victory. In his final game, his stat-line was also unspectacular: he completed just 13 passes for 141 yards as his defense and running back CJ Anderson did the damage in a 24-10 win over Cam Newton and the Carolina Panthers. But it didn't matter – Manning left the field a champion.

Ultimately, Manning will be remembered for many things – most positive and some negative – but he will certainly be remembered. There has perhaps never been a bigger brain in the pocket.

SWEETNESS AND FIGHT

A monster on the field and a gentleman off it, Walter Payton brought the stiff-arm back into fashion and the Bears back to respectability

WALTER PAYTON

POSITION: Running Back
NFL DRAFT: 1975/Round 1/Pick 4
CAREER: Chicago Bears (1975-1987)
····
HIGHLIGHTS:
Super Bowl Champion (XX)
9 x Pro Bowl (1976-1980, 1984, 1985)
2 x NFC Offensive Player of the Year (1977, 1985)
NFL Offensive Player of the Year (1977)
NFL Rushing YardsLeader (1977)
NFL Rushing Touchdowns Leader (1977)
NFL 1970s All-Decade Team
NFL 1980s All-Decade Team
NFL 75th Anniversary All-Time Team
16,726 Career Rushing Yards
110Career Rushing Touchdowns
15 Career Receiving Touchdowns
Pro Football Hall of Fame (Enshrined 1993)

R unning backs in high school generally fall into two categories. They are either shifty slashers or straight-ahead bowling balls of butcher's knives. Walter Payton was both. He ran hard on every play, never stopped churning his arms and pumping his knees. His stiff-arm, which had fallen out of fashion, was developed on the dust-bowls of Jefferson, Mississippi, and it could incapacitate opposing defenders.

A content Walter Payton on the sidelines in October 1985

BEARS — RUNNING BACK — WALTER PAYTON — 34

The stiff-arm was brought back into fashion by 'Sweetness'

PLAZA

C | 118 | 07 | 02
GATE | SECTION | ROW | SEAT

SUPER BOWL XX

NFL

AFC-NFC WORLD CHAMPIONSHIP GAME
Sunday, January 26, 1986   Kickoff 4:00 P.M.
Louisiana Superdome $75.00

Sunday, January 26, 1986
Kickoff 4:00 P.M.   Gates Open 1:00 P.M.
$75.00   All taxes included

GATE | SECTION | ROW | SEAT

C | 118 | 07 | 02

His hips rarely locked into one position and he relished using a defender's movement against him. In his autobiography, he wrote: "I began to see that once in a great while you can use getting hit to keep your balance. It's all a matter of reflexes and coordination and eyes and hands and feet."

He was a natural athlete, even breaking the state championship long jump record. His Adonis-chiselled torso, long arms, thick calves and thighs like fire hydrants, were gifts from the Gods. Yet he still needed coaching.

Robert Hill was a drill-sergeant head coach, promoted to the top job at Jackson State in December 1970. Payton knew of his hothead reputation, and because of it had mixed feelings about going there. His players nicknamed him 'Thirst' – for bloodthirsty.

Yet Hill must be credited for two things: teaching Payton how to block, and how to run. At nights when the other players were at home watching TV or studying, Hill dragged Payton to Jackson State's gymnasium, where he hung a tackling dummy from a steel beam. Payton pounded that dummy until it was even more sore than he was.

Though larger and stronger than his older brother Eddie, the featured back who was used to recruit his talented younger sibling out of Colombia High School, Walter tended to take hand-offs and break to the outside. It worked in high school, where he was faster than most cornerbacks and safeties, but he could not get away with it each time in college. Hill was riled by Walter's tendency to break for the outside. Stopping practice one day, Hill called for Willie Swinning, the team's trainer. In earshot of Walter, he handed Swinning a bag and shouted: "Fill this up with three or four bricks."

Swinning placed four footballs into the bag when no-one was looking and gave it to Hill, who called for a drill involving a hand-off from the quarterback to the running back. Like clockwork, Walter broke for the outside. Hill charged forward, swinging the bag wildly toward Payton's head. "Back inside!" Hill bellowed "Get your ass back inside!"

Payton bowed out with a 6-3 win over the LA Raiders at the Los Angeles Memorial Coliseum

He repeated the drill, over and over. "It took him a couple of times with me swinging that bag of bricks," said Hill, "but he finally started charging into the hole. That's how he began running inside."

He also got Payton out of the habit of running with raised knees, as he felt that knees close to the body made it easier for a tackler to grab everything at once. Hill advised Payton to run with long strides and extended legs, which made it harder for a tackler and led to more explosive runs. His long-striding gait was powered largely by his hips. It served him well and his legend grew with a seven-touchdown showing in a 72-0 rout of Lane College in Payton's sophomore year, where he set a new Jackson State mark of 279 rushing yards.

Payton completed his undergraduate course work in three years and was at ease when beginning his 1974-75 senior academic year. The Tigers were ridiculously talented, returning 38 lettermen and a fully intact offensive line. Though he rushed for 1,029 yards, 13 touchdowns, kicked a field goal and six extra points, the Tigers finished with a 7-3 record and Payton finished just 14th in the Heisman Trophy race. He ended with 3,563 yards and scored 464 points at Jackson State, where he earned the name 'Sweetness' because of his smooth-running style.

In 1975, Payton was drafted by the 4-10 Chicago Bears, who had not posted a winning season since 1967. He was bypassed by the Dallas Cowboys, who had the second pick. Payton wanted to go there and was devastated, reportedly breaking down in tears that he had to go to Chicago, who had taken him with the fourth pick.

He was a ready-made replacement for Gayle Sayers. The Bears had desperately sought a running back since he retired in 1971. Strong, fast, rugged, powerful – in Payton the Bears finally got what they wanted, inking a three-year deal that paid him $150,000 annually, with a $126,000 signing bonus, four months after the draft.

The offensive line for the Bears was an ode to mediocrity, however, and Payton gained zero net yards on eight carries in an opening-day 35-7 defeat by the Colts. His rookie year was tough. Surrounded by second-rate talent, he managed 679 yards and seven touchdowns, with 134 yards in his final game of the season against the New Orleans Saints. Things gradually improved for both Payton and the Bears. In 1976, his second season, he was elected to the Pro Bowl after a 1,390-yard, 13-touchdown campaign, and was the league's leading scorer with 16 touchdowns the following year, hitting a career-best 1,852 yards. His best single-game performance occurred on November 20, 1977, when he rushed for a barnstorming 275 yards against the Minnesota Vikings.

For 13 seasons with the Bears, Payton mesmerised observers with his spectacular play. He had the speed to run outside, plus the power to drive up the middle. Exceptionally durable, he missed only one game in his rookie season and then played 186 consecutive games. His astonishing durability helped him establish NFL records for carries (3,838), yards gained (16,726) and rushing touchdowns (110). A complete football player, he was a devastating blocker and caught 492 passes for 4,538 yards and 15 touchdowns.

Despite all the attention and honours bestowed upon him during his extraordinary career – which reached a peak with a 46-10 victory in Super Bowl XX over New England – Payton always maintained a healthy perspective. Upon learning of his election to the Hall of Fame, he humbly remarked: "I'm thrilled but embarrassed. I got paid for playing a kid's game, and I enjoyed it."

Despite being a punishing runner, Payton rarely ran out of bounds. He explained: "My coach at Jackson State, Bob Hill, always said that if you are going to die, you should die hard, never easy." Indeed, 'Never Die Easy' was the title of his posthumously published autobiography.

His death at the tender age of 45 from cholangiocarcinoma (bile duct cancer), on November 1, 1999, was certainly hard to take.

Yet his legacy is a rich one; it includes the Walter Payton Award, for the most outstanding offensive player in the Division 1 Football Championship Subdivision (formerly 1-AA) in college football, and The Walter Payton NFL Man of the Year Award, presented annually, honouring a player's volunteer and charity work.

SLIPPING THROUGH THE CRACKS

Walter Payton loved fast cars. He had been stopped for speeding in Chicago more than 50 times, yet almost always drove away with merely a warning. Yet in the autumn of 1992, an unsympathetic judge had ordered him to partake in six months of community service. He turned up at a Hoffman Estates High School, offering to volunteer his time to the Hawks basketball team. Payton took pride in not being a typical superstar athlete and this association continued. In 1995-96, the Hawks reached the Class AA state tournament in Peoria. Before the team left for the finals, Payton gave a pep talk about commitment and trust and what it means to be a champion. At the end of it, he slipped off his Super Bowl ring and handed it to centre Nick Abruzzo. He said: "Nick, I want you to hold on to the ring for the weekend. I trust you, just like you need to trust one another."

That night, Abruzzo held a party for teammates at his house and the ring went missing. Payton tried his best to play the incident down. However, he was heartbroken. Two years later the Abruzzo family moved and sold their old furniture. Philip Hong, a graduating senior, claimed the couch. One evening, in 2001, his dog, looking for a chew toy, ripped the lining on the underside. Hong stuck his arm beneath the couch to retrieve the ball, but instead grasped Payton's Super Bowl ring. He returned the jewellery to Connie. She gave him a framed photo of her late husband.

Payton rarely ran out of bounds, instead preferring to punish his opponents

Walter Payton lost the Super Bowl XX ring he won when the Bears defeated the Patriots 46-10 at the Superdome on January 26, 1986

A STARR IS BORN

Paired with coach Vince Lombardi, legendary quarterback Bart Starr overcame painful adversity to bring five championships to Green Bay

Starr warms up ahead of a regular season game against the San Francisco 49ers

BRYAN BARTLETT STARR

POSITION: Quarterback
NFL DRAFT: 1956/Round 17/Pick 200
CAREER: Green Bay Packers (1956-1971, Player)
Green Bay Packers (1975-1983, Head coach)
••••
HIGHLIGHTS:
2 x Super Bowl Champion (I, II)
3 x NFL Champion (1961, 1962, 1967)
2 x Super Bowl MVP (I, II)
4 x Pro Bowl (1960-1962, 1966)
NFL MVP (1966)
5 x NFL Passer Rating Leader (1962, 1964, 1966, 1968, 1969)
NFL 1960s All-Decade Team
1,808 career Pass completions
Career TD-INT: 152-138
24,718 Career Passing Yards
Pro Football Hall of Fame (Enshrined 1977)

Bart Starr lived with a secret for 62 years. He played and coached through chronic pain his entire career because of an incident of bullying. It was the nature of a very ugly beast.

He received a hazing so bad at the University of Alabama – beaten with a wooden paddle until his

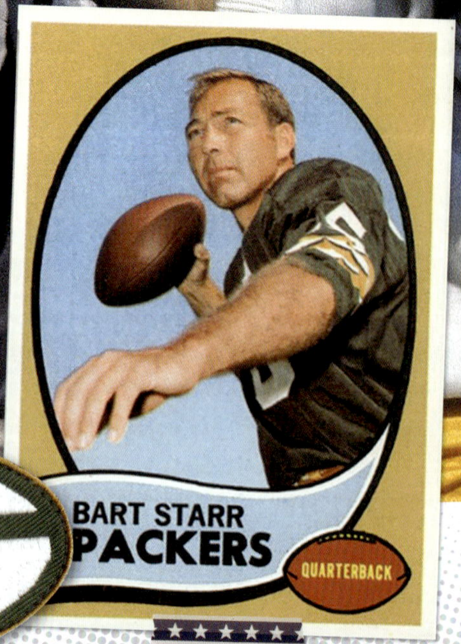

BART STARR
PACKERS

QUARTERBACK

Escaping pressure in the Packers' 35-10 win over Kansas City in Super Bowl I

He had to ask her four times before she finally said yes and when they eloped, she changed into her wedding dress inside a muddy service station in rural Mississippi.

The picture was painted that he struggled throughout his career at Alabama and never developed into a good quarterback until Vince Lombardi arrived in Green Bay in 1959. Yet Starr started his sophomore season, helped Alabama to an SEC championship and, entering his junior season, was hailed by his coach, Harold 'Red' Drew, as possibly the best passer in the Crimson Tide's history.

With Starr sidelined or playing through pain, Alabama finished 1954 with a record of 4-5-2 and went the final six games without a win. The following season, Hank Crisp replaced Drew with Jennings Whitworth, who was an advocate of a run-heavy attack.

Starr was benched for most of his junior season and Alabama went 0-10, the worst season in Crimson Tide history. Yet there were two defining moments that put Starr on the road to greatness with Green Bay. Firstly, he was drafted in the 17th round (200th overall) on a recommendation by Alabama's basketball coach Johnny Dee, who was a friend of Jack Vainisi, the personnel director of the Packers. Vainisi, who had persuaded the executive board to hire Lombardi from the New York Giants in 1958, also brought seven future Hall of Famers including Starr, Paul Hornung, Jim Taylor, Ray Nitschke, Forrest Gregg and Jim Ringo to Wisconsin. He died suddenly at the age of 33 in November 1960, from a chronic rheumatic condition that swelled his heart to twice its normal size. No question, he had one of the most underappreciated and exceptional careers in Pro Football.

Secondly, and perhaps the most amazing aspect of Starr's career, might be this. He was so badly beaten in the hazing that he failed his medical examination for the Air Force and was medically disqualified and discharged in the spring of 1957 after his rookie season in Green Bay.

The military said Starr was unfit for service. If Starr had a healthy back, he would have remained in the Air Force for at least two more years. As luck and determination would have it, he then played 15 more years in the NFL and won five championships, including the first two Super Bowls, and was named Most Valuable Player of both.

back was red raw – that it derailed his college career, disqualified him from military service and affected him constantly throughout his 16 years with the Green Bay Packers.

It had long been accepted that Starr hurt his back during a punting exercise. Five biographies and an autobiography published in 1987, craft a narrative around that story. Yet Starr buried the real reason for his injury in 1954 and his horrific beating at the hands of the A-Club fraternity – which had him in traction for a week – because, according to his wife Cherry, "he thought it would make him look bad".

"His back was never right after that," she said. "It was horrible. It was not a football injury. It was an injury sustained from hazing. It was so brutal."

Starr suffered the worst of it before his junior season, and only a few months after he eloped with Cherry, when they were just 20. In 1954, teams used to revoke or reduce scholarships for marriages, but he also had the temerity to wed an Auburn girl and take her to Tuscaloosa.

THE ICE BOWL HERO

The game-time temperature at Lambeau Field was about −26°C, with an average wind chill of around −44°C. At one point, CBS announcer Frank Gifford said on air: "I'm going to take a bite out of my coffee." Seven members of the University of Wisconsin-La Crosse marching band were taken to hospital with hypothermia. Instruments stuck to lips or froze completely. One elderly spectator died from exposure. The 1967 NFL Championship Game, played on December 31, pitted Dallas, the Eastern Conference winners, against the Packers, the Western Conference winners, for a place in Super Bowl II. It was a rematch of the previous year's title game and dubbed 'The Ice Bowl', the game that defined Bart Starr's career. In their last offensive drive, the Packers, trailing 17-14, took over possession at their own 32-yard line with 4:50 left in regulation time. Starr, who called all the plays, moved them to third-and-goal at the Dallas two-foot line with just 16 seconds remaining and went to the sidelines to confer with Vince Lombardi.

According to Starr, he said: "Coach, the linemen can get their footing for the Wedge, but the backs are slipping. I'm right there, I can just lunge in." A frozen Lombardi told Starr: "Run it, and let's get the hell out of here!" Brown right 31 Wedge was a play designed for the full-back, but Starr did not tell his teammates he was keeping the ball, and executed it perfectly. He plunged over. The extra point made it 21-17 and the Packers advanced, going on to defeat the Oakland Raiders 33-14 in Super Bowl II.

A packed crowd watched the game play out despite the sub-zero temperatures

Lombardi's first impression of Starr, he acknowledged, was that "he was probably just a little too polite and maybe just a little too self-effacing to be the real bold tough quarterback that a quarterback must be in the National Football league". Starr felt otherwise and was determined to prove himself to Lombardi, no matter how long it took. "I could see in my own mind, day by day, week by week, that this was going to be a lengthy process because trust and respect should never just be handed out to somebody," Starr said later. "You have to earn it".

The more Starr studied Lombardi's system, the more he felt he could flourish in it. Endless hours of film study in the classroom environment, analysing plays, set Starr apart. "I loved it. Loved the meetings. I never, ever was bored or tired in any meeting we were in with Lombardi. I appreciated what he was trying to teach. He was always raising the bar."

If anyone could handle Lombardi's methods, it was Bart Starr. After what he had endured at home with this father, Lombardi's treatment would seem benign.

Ben Starr was a stern military man who drilled his sons Bryan Bartlett 'Bart' and Hilton 'Bubba', in the practice of obedience and respect for elders. No matter how he tried, Bart felt he could not win his father's love and respect, and Bubba was evidently considered the vessel of his father's ambitions. Things got infinitely worse for Bart when Bubba died at the age of 13. He had been playing barefoot in a vacant field and was cut on the heel by an old dog bone. He died of tetanus three days later and his mother was wracked by guilt thereafter for being reluctant to bring him in for a shot that would have saved his life.

Starr had shown flashes of brilliance when given an opportunity to play quarterback late in Lombardi's first year, but then regressed and was benched again after the 1960 opening day loss to the Bears. "That was a real wake-up call for me," said Starr. "I had let him down. So, I was more determined than ever to get it back."

When the time came again, as the Packers drove towards the conference crown, Starr was mentally and physically ready. It helped that he'd stood up to Lombardi after the coach exploded at him in front of teammates following in interception in practice. Starr explained that the ball had been tipped, and the coach was wrong in also "chewing

Dropping back to pass against the St Louis Cardinals

A back injury, the result of a brutal hazing, troubled Starr throughout his career

"Starr hungered for Lombardi's sense of order and football knowledge, and Lombardi knew he had a quarterback who was loyal in every way"

my butt out in front of the team you want me to lead". The challenge had worked. Lombardi never criticised him in front of them again. Starr said later: "From then on, we had a relationship that was just unbelievable. I don't think it had been that bad before, but now it just took off and went to another plane."

Starr hungered for Lombardi's sense of order and football knowledge, and Lombardi knew he had a quarterback who was loyal in every way. Together they built a dynasty.

The Packers advanced to the 1960 NFL Championship game but lost to the Philadelphia Eagles, Lombardi's only post-season loss as a head coach. They returned to the title game and won in 1961 and 1962, overcoming the New York Giants on both occasions.

Then they became the only team to win three consecutive titles in 1965-67, the last victory coming in Super Bowl II against the Oakland Raiders. Lombardi stepped down afterwards. Starr had also originally planned to retire after the Super Bowl win in January 1968, but without a clear successor and a new head coach, he stayed on, although was subsequently limited by elbow surgeries and retired after the 1971 season, having posted the second-best career passer-rating of 80.5.

There is a back story to his career. Quite literally. After he had retired as head coach of the Packers, following nine largely unsuccessful years in 1983 (the first five as

his own general manager), Cherry and Bart moved to Birmingham, Alabama. That was when a small fissure, a nearly undetectable crack, was discovered in one of Starr's vertebrae. According to Cherry, the fracture was "basically invisible" and located on the anterior side of her husband's spine. Starr had surgery to "remove a chip" and the chronic pain, which had plagued him since he was 20, alleviated.

Starr's celebrated career is therefore even more remarkable, since in all likelihood, he played throughout with a broken back.

Bart Starr's No. 15 jersey is one of just six retired by the Packers

THE INNOVATOR

How the unprecedented career of Green Bay receiver Don Hutson changed the course of football

The four-times NFL All-Star also led the league in interceptions in 1940

DON HUTSON

POSITION: Split End
CAREER: Green Bay Packers (1935-1945)
••••
HIGHLIGHTS:
3 x NFL Champion (1936, 1939, 1944)
4 x NFL All-Star (1939-1942)
2 x NFL Most Valuable Player (1941, 1942)
8 x NFL Receptions Leader (1936, 1938, 1939, 1941-1945)
7 x NFL Receiving Yards Leader (1936, 1938, 1939, 1941-1944)
9 x NFL Receiving Touchdowns Leader (1935-1938, 1940-1944)
NFL Interceptions Leader (1940)
99 Career Receiving Touchdowns
NFL 75th Anniversary All-Time Team
NFL 1930s All-Decade Team
Pro Football Hall of Fame (Enshrined 1963)

ALABAMA
58
ALL AMERICAN

DON HUTSON   End

Sport deals only in excessive simplicities. True, you may find everywhere examples of subtlety of execution: a free-kick around a wall, a forehand down the line or a zone block. But there can never be subtlety of achievement. You win or you don't win; such a matter cannot be oversimplified.

Likewise, much of the study of history is a matter of comparison, of relating what was happening in one era to what was happening elsewhere, and what had happened in the past. To view a period in isolation is to miss whatever message it has to offer.

Yet there can be no mistake about Don Hutson. You could compare him to any player of any era and come up with the same conclusion: he was a the most dominant single player from his position in history. He changed the way the game was played and he was a winner.

While speed was a vital element to the 6ft 1", 185-pound Hutson, he was also a hard-worker. The

14

Packers coach Curly Lambeau with RB Tony Canadeo (3), QB Irv Comp (51) and Hutson (14)

Dubbed the 'Alabama Antelope', Hutson was named to All-America teams in 1933, his junior year, and in 1934 when Alabama claimed its fourth national championship, his senior year. In that Rose Bowl, the Crimson Tide completed a perfect 10-0 season with an upset of much-fancied Stanford, with the 21-year-old catching touchdown passes of 50 and 59 yards.

Green Bay Packers head coach Curly Lambeau liked speed. He had brought John 'Blood' McNally back to his native Wisconsin in 1929 and the half-back enjoyed eight fruitful years a key member on four world championship teams. Blood was one of the fastest men in football, with the same swivel-hip changes of direction that made Red Grange an electrifying runner.

Lambeau saw similarities in the fleet-footed Hutson, who could run the 100-yard dash in 9.7 seconds, and had the deep pockets to get him. He became the perfect complement to Blood and strong-armed quarterback Arnie Herber, who joined Green Bay in 1930.

Herber reached his peak in 1935 with Hutson's arrival. The league's first true wide receiver made his mark with his first professional reception – an 83-yard touchdown pass from Herber on the first play of the game when the Packers beat the Chicago Bears 7-0. George Halas, the Bears' coach, said: "For the next ten years Hutson was doing that sort of thing to every club in the National Football League. I just concede him two touchdowns a game and I hope we can score more."

Hutson's first season was remarkable. He set new records with 34 catches, 526 yards receiving and eight touchdowns, all marks that he would soon eclipse. He helped Herber to a record 177 passes for 1,239 yards and 11 touchdowns. The Packers finished

quiet, genial figure once said: "For every pass I caught in a game, I caught a thousand in practice."

Hutson was dedicated to the mechanics of perfection, undertaking a remorseless, intransigent training regime. He was also a genuine purveyor of intuitive, disquieting brilliance. He could be relied upon in a crisis – and at a cocktail party.

Few sportsmen have dominated over such a long period and he practically invented the modern receiving game, ushering in the passing era of pro football. Other split ends ran straight to a spot and then waited. Hutson created Z-outs, button-hooks, the hook-and-go, and a whole catalogue of moves and fakes. No other player impacted the game as much as Donald Montgomery Hutson.

Born on January 31, 1913 in Pine Bluff, Arkansas, Hutson played football for just one year in high school and only went to the University of Alabama because Bob Seawall, a high school teammate refused to go unless the Crimson Tide would take Hutson, too.

While Seawall dropped out after two years, Hutson became an icon, more celebrated than the other starting end Paul 'Bear' Bryant, who went on to become one of the game's legendary coaches. The pair were not just partners on the field. Off it, they were partners in a campus dry-cleaning service.

"He practically invented the modern receiving game, ushering in the passing era of pro football"

Hutson in action against the New York Giants in the 1938 championship game

10-1-1 and went to the NFL title game, which they won 21-6 over the Boston Redskins at the Polo Grounds in New York, with Hutson grabbing one touchdown pass.

He also played both ways, on offense and defense. Widely regarded as the league's top safety, he was accredited with 30 career interceptions, even though they were not recorded as a statistic until his sixth NFL season. He also handled extra points and field goals from time-to-time. He successfully kicked 94% of his career point-after attempts when 80% was considered the norm.

Two more titles for the Packers followed in 1939 and 1944, and he led the league in receptions and touchdowns eight times before retiring following the 1945 season.

Hutson was a nine-time All-Pro and won two league MVP trophies in 11 seasons with the Packers.

Despite playing in seasons that numbered only 11 or 12 games most years, Hutson is still in the Top 100 in NFL history in receiving yards (7,991, 93rd), receiving yards per game (68.9, 29th), yards per reception (16.4, 85th), points scored (823, 88th), touchdown receptions (99, 11th) and overall touchdowns (105, 21st).

However, a little context on Hutson's remarkable career is required. The Great Depression had stoked an increase in racism and self-inflicted segregation across the country. From 1934 to 1945, there were no black players in the league. The lockout of black players can also be attributed to the entry of George Preston Marshall into the league in 1932. He openly refused to have black athletes on his Boston Braves/Washington Redskins teams, and reportedly pressured the rest of the league to follow suit. The NFL did not have another black player until after World War II.

Yet it must also be remembered that Hutson produced incredible stats in an era when the average passer rating was in the mid-40s, when there were no facemasks and receivers could be hit all the way down the field. There was no such thing as a receiver wearing gloves or covering himself in Stickum. This was also in an era in which teams often passed only on third down, and only when they needed long yardage for a first down.

Modern-day comparisons are difficult, but not impossible. You could certainly compare Hutson to those in the first 25 years of NFL history, where he is head and shoulders above everyone in terms of speed, production, toughness and versatility.

The receiving touchdowns total stood as the NFL record for 44 years until Steve Largent broke it in 1989. Every other player now in the top 10 in career receiving touchdowns began his career after 1984.

And one of every 4.9 of Hutson's receptions went for a touchdown. Jerry Rice, by comparison, who nabbed 197 receiving touchdowns, scored on one of every 7.8 catches in his career.

Hutson was rightly proud of the 18 records he set when retiring, and in 2017 still holds the records for most seasons leading the league in receptions (eight), most consecutive seasons leading in receptions (five), most seasons leading in touchdowns (eight), most seasons leading in scoring (five) and most points scored in a quarter (29). Still, he maintained: "I love to see my records broken, I really do – you get a chance to relive your life, the whole experience."

When he retired, he had three times as many touchdowns as any receiver in the first 25 years of pro football and was earning $15,000 a year, a huge sum. His skills were still evident, but he said: "It was playing defense that wore me out."

He spent two years as an assistant coach of the Packers and then became a wealthy owner of an auto dealership and bowling lanes in Racine, Wisconsin.

A charter member of the Pro Football Hall of Fame in 1963, the Packers retired his No. 14 jersey in 1951 and he also had a street named after him. Hutson moved to Rancho Mirage, California, after retiring from business, and died there on June 26, 1997, at the age of 84.

Packers' GM Ron Wolf may have been a little understated when he said: "He most certainly was the greatest player in the history of this franchise."

For arguably, Don Hutson is the greatest player in the history of the game.

TWO CONTRACTS, ONE DRAFT

If there was one player responsible for the NFL Draft, it was Hutson. In December 1934, ahead of the Rose Bowl between Alabama and Stanford, deep pockets became ripped pockets for Green Bay Packers coach Curly Lambeau.

As fate would have it, he tied Peyton Manning's record for most career passing touchdowns (539) with another pass to Tre'Quan Smith in December 2019, breaking the record later on in the same game.

Each year he would go to Pasadena, California, to scout prospects in college football's title game, the Rose Bowl. On this occasion, Lambeau was barred from watching Alabama's secret practice, so he scaled a wall to watch, ripping his trousers in the process.

Lambeau was suitably impressed by what he saw in the flesh and Hutson confirmed Lambeau's view when catching seven passes, two for touchdowns, in Alabama's 29-13 upset over Stanford on New Year's Day, 1935. Hutson quickly received offers to join the professional ranks.

He said: "I had letters from maybe ten pro clubs. I ended up going to Green Bay because the Packers offered the most money – $300 a game. That was far and above what they ever paid a player."

In fact, Hutson signed two contracts.

Jim "Shipwreck" Kelly, co-owner of the Brooklyn Dodgers, got Hutson to ink a similar deal to Lambeau's. Joe Carr, the NFL president, decreed that whichever team lodged the contract first, would get Hutson. Lambeau's won, by dint of a slightly earlier postmark.

A year later, to avoid instances of players signing for two teams, the NFL decided to have a draft for the first time.

Hutson (left) and Dixie Howell are awarded All-America honours in 1933

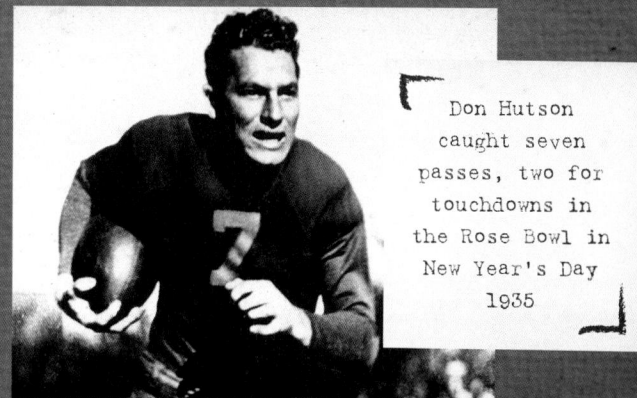

Don Hutson caught seven passes, two for touchdowns in the Rose Bowl in New Year's Day 1935

THE SAVIOUR

The triggerman for the Triplets was everything Cowboys dreamed he would be

SUPER BOWL XXVII

GATE C 03 | TUNNEL | ROW J | SEAT 109

AFC-NFC World Championship Game
SUNDAY, JANUARY 31, 1993 · 3:00 PM
Rose Bowl · Pasadena, California

$175 ALL TAXES INCLUDED
Gates Open At 12:00 PM

Pasadena

AFC-NFC World Championship Game
SUNDAY, JANUARY 31, 1993 · 3:00 PM
Rose Bowl · Pasadena, California

$175 ALL TAXES INCLUDED

TROY AIKMAN

POSITION: Quarterback
NFL DRAFT: 1989/Round 1/Pick 1
CAREER: Dallas Cowboys (1989-2000)
• • • •
HIGHLIGHTS:
3 x Super Bowl Champion (XXVII, XXVIII, XXX)
Super Bowl MVP (XXVII)
6 x Pro Bowl (1991-1996)
NFL Man of the Year (1996)
Career TD-INT: 165-141
32,942 Career Passing Yards
61.5 Career Completion %
Pro Football Hall of Fame (Enshrined 2006)

TROY AIKMAN
DALLAS COWBOYS · QB

Not every No. 1 draft pick is a success. Examples include Tim Couch, David Carr, Aundray Bruce, Courtney Brown, Tom Cousineau, JaMarcus Russell and Ki-Jana Carter. In the case of Troy Aikman, who went to Dallas in 1989 as the top overall draft choice and the team's first pick under owner Jerry Jones and coach Jimmy Johnson, he was everything the franchise expected. Immediately labelled the team's saviour, he sure enough helped the Cowboys once again become the NFL's most loved and loathed team. Aikman was the triggerman in an offense that also featured running back Emmitt Smith and receiver Michael Irvin. The 'Triplets' propelled Dallas to the top of the NFL three seasons after it was at the bottom, and they

The clean-cut Aikman won an MVP award for his display in Super Bowl XXVII against Buffalo

claimed an unprecedented three Super Bowls in four years, including successive titles in 1992 and 1993. Aikman was the MVP of the first, a 52-17 victory over Buffalo.

A strong-armed, accurate passer, Aikman made quick reads and had the intelligence to throw the ball exactly where it needed to be. He had a style that coaches loved.

His third Super Bowl, in January 1996, came under Barry Switzer, who coached the Cowboys for four years after Johnson was fired. A thorough professional on and off the field, Aikman barely enjoyed that season, dismayed by Switzer allowing players to miss practices at training camp. According to several sources, Aikman and Switzer barely spoke during the 1996 and 1997 seasons, as the aging Cowboys, still one of the most talented teams, began to fall apart.

Aikman retired after 12 seasons – and 10 concussions – at the age of 34, following a persistent back injury, but his subsequent television career as a sportscaster for the Fox network has brought him wide praise.

Many younger viewers will hold Richard Sherman's cornerback play within the Seattle Seahawks infamous 'Legion of Boom' in the highest regard. His game-winning interception in the NFC Championship game against the San Francisco 49ers in 2013 was followed by a spectacular on-camera rant about wide receiver Michael Crabtree and how Sherman was the self proclaimed 'best corner in the game.'

"Immediately labelled the team's saviour, he sure enough helped the Cowboys once again become the NFL's most loved and loathed team."

10 GREATEST NFL GAMES OF ALL TIME

Home to some of the biggest sporting contests in history, the NFL is proof positive of how impactful sport can be at its best

There's a reason the NFL is one of the world's most watched sporting leagues. Showcasing an athletic spectacle that manages to capture the imagination of even the most casual fan, it has been responsible for some truly memorable moments since its inception in 1920. Year after year in the NFL, heroes are born and legends are made, and the actions of both individuals and teams have contributed to some truly stunning contests.

From records being broken to underdogs upsetting the odds, the NFL has played host to some spectacular games down the years. They're milestones of the sporting world that deserve recognition, not only because of the outstanding skill on display, but because of the emotional resonance that these sporting achievements hold for so many people. With all that in mind, over the next few pages we present ten of the very best NFL games ever played for your reading pleasure.

SUPER BOWL LI

Confetti rains down on the
stadium after the New England
Patriots defeat the Atlanta Falcons
in Super Bowl 51

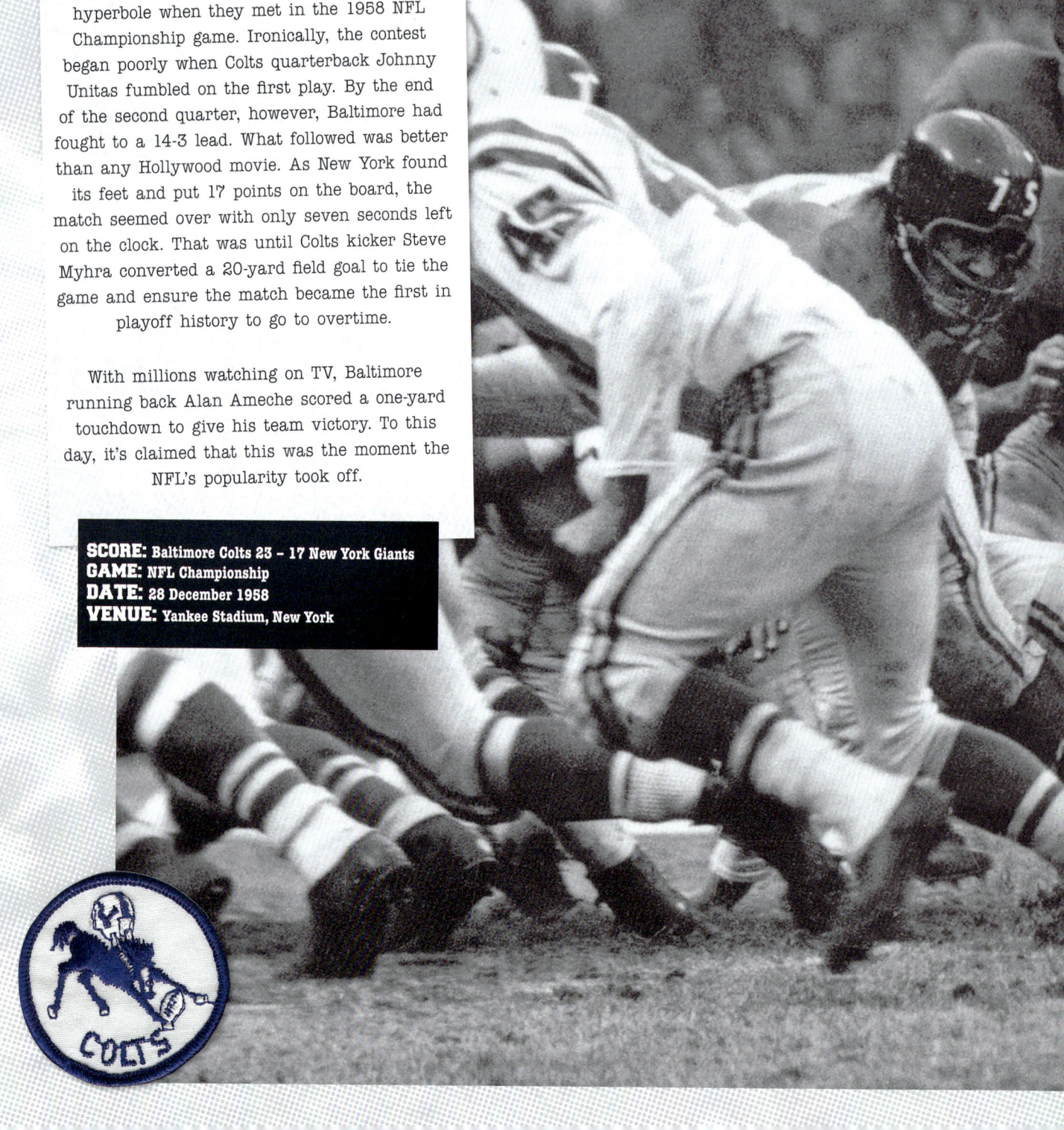

'THE GREATEST GAME EVER PLAYED'

01 When a game is dubbed 'the greatest ever', it's natural to take the statement with a grain of salt.

Fortunately, the Baltimore Colts and New York Giants did more than enough to justify such hyperbole when they met in the 1958 NFL Championship game. Ironically, the contest began poorly when Colts quarterback Johnny Unitas fumbled on the first play. By the end of the second quarter, however, Baltimore had fought to a 14-3 lead. What followed was better than any Hollywood movie. As New York found its feet and put 17 points on the board, the match seemed over with only seven seconds left on the clock. That was until Colts kicker Steve Myhra converted a 20-yard field goal to tie the game and ensure the match became the first in playoff history to go to overtime.

With millions watching on TV, Baltimore running back Alan Ameche scored a one-yard touchdown to give his team victory. To this day, it's claimed that this was the moment the NFL's popularity took off.

SCORE: Baltimore Colts 23 – 17 New York Giants
GAME: NFL Championship
DATE: 28 December 1958
VENUE: Yankee Stadium, New York

The New York Giants defend against the Baltimore Colts during the 1958 NFL Championship game at Yankee Stadium on December 28, 1958

YANKEE STADIUM
161st ST. and RIVER AVE., N.Y.C.
KICK-OFF
2:05 P.M.
NATIONAL FOOTBALL LEAGUE
1958 WORLD'S CHAMPIONSHIP
NEW YORK GIANTS VS
BALTIMORE COLTS
THIS TICKET CANNOT BE SOLD FOR MORE THAN THE PRICE NAMED HEREON,
MANAGEMENT RESERVES THE RIGHT TO REVOKE THIS LICENSE BY REFUNDING MONEY.
BERT BELL
COMMISIONER

YANKEE STADIUM
1958 WORLD'S CHAMPIONSHIP
LOWER
BOX SEAT
$10.00
NO REFUND

THE 100-YARD INTERCEPTION

02 **Records are meant to be broken, but in 2009 during Super Bowl XLIII, Pittsburgh Steelers outside linebacker James Harrison set one in the most dramatic fashion possible.** After Arizona Cardinals quarterback Kurt Warner's wayward pass ended up in the arms of Harrison in his own end zone, he ran 100 yards for a then-record interception return touchdown. Aside from highlighting just how in-sync and well-oiled the Steelers were as a team – everyone on the field did everything they could to clear Harrison's path – it also sent them into half-time with a 17-7 lead.

This alone would have been enough to make Super Bowl XLIII a game to remember, but Arizona returned to the field with renewed purpose. While they struggled in the third quarter, things picked up in the fourth. Warner, wanting to make up for his earlier error, inspired his team to 16 consecutive points, including wide receiver Larry Fitzgerald's 64-yard touchdown reception. It took the game to 23-20 with only 2:37 remaining. It was quickly becoming a game of one-upmanship, but there was yet another twist to come.

It appeared the Cardinals had cemented a terrific comeback, but Steelers quarterback Ben Roethlisberger had other ideas. Working near-perfectly with wide receiver Santonio Holmes, who he found four times in a 78-yard drive, Big Ben found Holmes for the game-winning touchdown with a pass that many consider one of the best ever thrown in a Super Bowl. With the championship secured, Pittsburgh became the first team in history to win six Super Bowls, adding yet another record to the books.

A game full of highlights that are still exhilarating to watch today, Super Bowl XLIII managed to secure 98.7 million viewers, making it one of the most watched events in broadcast history. Easily one of the best finals that the NFL has ever witnessed, it's a contest that gets better every time you watch it.

SCORE: Pittsburgh Steelers 27 – 23 Arizona Cardinals
GAME: Super Bowl XLIII
DATE: 1 February 2009
VENUE: Raymond James Stadium, Tampa, FL

NAMATH'S JETS DEFY THE ODDS

03 **Nothing beats a good underdog story.** Before Super Bowl III, everyone had predicted a walkover victory for the dominant Baltimore Colts. Part of the NFL – which was considered the superior league – the Colts had crushed their opposition that year, finishing the 1968 season with a record of 13-1. On the flip-side were the AFL's New York Jets. Fighting their way to the main event with far less momentum, the Jets squeaked their way through to the Super Bowl thanks to a 27-23 win over the Oakland Raiders. On paper, there was only going to be one champion that year.

So when Jets quarterback Joe Namath came out three days prior to the event to arrogantly declare his team would win, everyone took it for what they assumed it was: big words from a man who knew his team didn't have a chance. As it turned out, he couldn't have been more right.

Not only did the Jets control most of the game, but by the fourth quarter they had built up a 16-0 lead. Even more surprising was that they only scored one touchdown throughout the game – provided by running back Matt Snell – a Super Bowl final record that still holds true to this day (the rest of the Jets' points were provided thanks to three field goals by kicker Jim Turner). By the time Colts running back Jerry Hill pulled a touchdown back in the closing minutes, the damage had already been done.

Namath walked away as the game's MVP, completing 17 out of 28 passes for a total of 206 yards, even without throwing a single pass in the last quarter, since he knew well that it was better to err on the side of caution than give up what was a significant lead. The Jets had systemically picked holes in the Colts' defense. It was a historic night for all involved, and a game that any fan owes it to themselves to see.

SCORE: New York Jets 16 – 7 Baltimore Colts
GAME: Super Bowl III
DATE: 12 January 1969
VENUE: Orange Bowl, Miami, FL

No one could've predicted before the game how intense a match Super Bowl XLIII would've become

Jets quarterback Joe Namath

AN IMPERFECT PERFECT RECORD

04 **It all seemed hopeless for the New York Giants.** Not only had their Super Bowl opponents the New England Patriots gone unbeaten for the entire season with a record of 18-0, but they were the heavy favourites in the biggest game of the year. With the score 14-10 in favour of the Patriots late in the fourth quarter, however, New York embarked on a drive that would not only earn them the Super Bowl that year, but cement this game as one of the biggest upsets in NFL history.

With the ball on their own 17-yard line and just 2:37 left on the clock, the Giants battled almost the entire length of the field to score a game-winning touchdown when wide receiver Plaxico Burress planted the ball down with only 35 seconds remaining. 97.5 million people tuned in to what many consider to be one of the best Super Bowls in history.

SCORE: New York Giants 17 – 14 New England Patriots
GAME: Super Bowl XLII
DATE: 3 February 2008
VENUE: University Of Phoenix Stadium, AZ

Super XLII was the first of two victories over the Patriots by the Giants and quarterback Eli Manning

Patrick Mahomes was named Super Bowl MVP, but he was helped by an impressive offensive line performance

SUPER BOWL SHOOTOUT

05 **The Super Bowl matchup at the end of the 2022 season was highly anticipated.** It featured the two teams with the league's best regular season records – both were 14-3 – and both had impressive quarterbacks, in Kansas City's MVP Patrick Mahomes and Philadelphia's breakout star Jalen Hurts. And the game didn't disappoint. The Eagles raced into a 24-14 lead at half-time, but the Chiefs worked their way back into it and took the lead in the fourth quarter when Kadarius Toney scored with a five-yard pass. Surely the game was over when Skyy Moore scored from a four-yard pass a few minutes later?

It wasn't. Hurts rushed into the end zone, then did the same again for a two-point conversion to tie the score. With second to go, Harrison Butker kicked a field goal to break Philly hearts and hand the Chiefs their second title under Mahomes and head coach Andy Reid.

SCORE: Kansas City Chiefs 38 – 35 Philadelphia Eagles
GAME: Super Bowl LXVII
DATE: 12 February 2023
VENUE: State Farm Stadium, Glendale, AZ

THE IMMACULATE RECEPTION

06 **The 'Immaculate Reception' is one of the most famous plays in NFL history.** Why? Mostly because it still creates controversy today. With the Oakland Raiders ahead in the dying seconds of the fourth quarter, the 1972 AFC divisional playoff seemed done and dusted. When Steelers quarterback Terry Bradshaw launched a pass to running back John Fuqua, though, everything changed.

Depending on who you choose to believe, the ball either bounced off Fuqua, the ground or Raiders safety Jack Tatum. The officials decided it was the last of these, allowing Pittsburgh fullback Franco Harris to grab the ball and run into the end zone to score a TD and ultimately win the game.

Some fans still contend that either Fuqua or the turf interfered first. If that were the case, the pass should have been ruled as incomplete. Given the contention, this face-off remains a treat to watch, if only to continually observe the game-changing play and wonder what might have been had it been called differently.

Regardless, this dispute did wonders for the Steelers. Not only did it secure their first playoff win ever, but it fuelled them to four Super Bowl victories before the decade was done. If the call had gone the other way, who knows what fate would have awaited the 'Men of Steel'.

SCORE: Oakland Raiders 7 – 13 Pittsburgh Steelers
GAME: AFC divisional playoff
DATE: 23 December 1972
VENUE: Three Rivers Stadium, Pittsburgh, PA

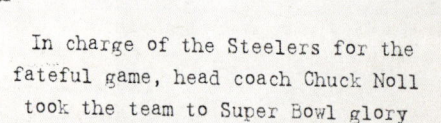

In charge of the Steelers for the fateful game, head coach Chuck Noll took the team to Super Bowl glory

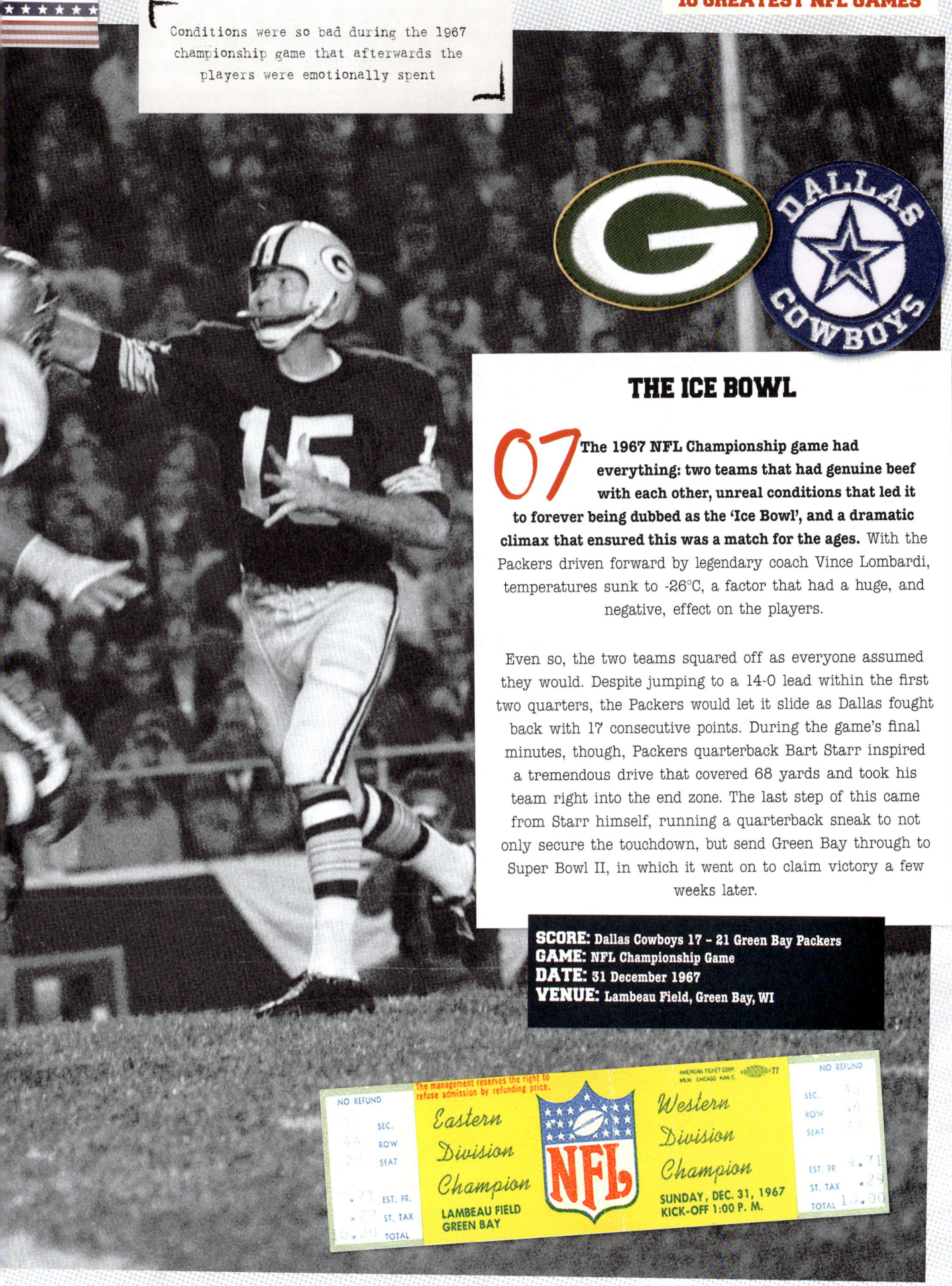

Conditions were so bad during the 1967 championship game that afterwards the players were emotionally spent

THE ICE BOWL

07 **The 1967 NFL Championship game had everything: two teams that had genuine beef with each other, unreal conditions that led it to forever being dubbed as the 'Ice Bowl', and a dramatic climax that ensured this was a match for the ages.** With the Packers driven forward by legendary coach Vince Lombardi, temperatures sunk to -26°C, a factor that had a huge, and negative, effect on the players.

Even so, the two teams squared off as everyone assumed they would. Despite jumping to a 14-0 lead within the first two quarters, the Packers would let it slide as Dallas fought back with 17 consecutive points. During the game's final minutes, though, Packers quarterback Bart Starr inspired a tremendous drive that covered 68 yards and took his team right into the end zone. The last step of this came from Starr himself, running a quarterback sneak to not only secure the touchdown, but send Green Bay through to Super Bowl II, in which it went on to claim victory a few weeks later.

SCORE: Dallas Cowboys 17 – 21 Green Bay Packers
GAME: NFL Championship Game
DATE: 31 December 1967
VENUE: Lambeau Field, Green Bay, WI

The management reserves the right to refuse admission by refunding price.

NO REFUND

Eastern Division Champion

NFL

LAMBEAU FIELD GREEN BAY

Western Division Champion

SUNDAY, DEC. 31, 1967 KICK-OFF 1:00 P. M.

SAN DIEGO CHARGERS

Garo Yepremian's kick finally secured the win for the Dolphins

SCORE: San Diego Chargers 41 – 38 Miami Dolphins
GAME: AFC divisional playoff
DATE: 2 January 1982
VENUE: Orange Bowl, Miami, FL

THE EPIC IN MIAMI

08 By the end of the first quarter, the San Diego Chargers were up 24-0 in their AFC divisional playoff against the Miami Dolphins. To say the world wrote the Dolphins off at that point would be an understatement – the feeling in the Orange Bowl was one of embarrassment. Until the second quarter, that is. After Dolphins head coach Don Shula switched quarterback David Woodley out for Don Strock, the game took a drastic turn. Opening his account with a 17-yard pass to Duriel Harris, this play also resulted in Miami's first points after a 34-yard field goal was converted by kicker Uwe von Schamann. From there it was all-out war.

By the end of the third quarter the Dolphins had, quite incredibly, managed to score 31 points. It took a touchdown from Chargers running back James Brooks with only 58 seconds left on the clock to tie the game and, even more spectacularly, a last-second field goal block from Chargers tight end Kellen Winslow to take things through to overtime.

While the Chargers would go on to win this divisional playoff game, the sheer drama and number of records set in one evening is what makes it an all-time classic, now known as the 'Epic in Miami'.

A last-minute field goal block would take the game to overtime

THE LONGEST GAME IN NFL HISTORY

09 Game length is not necessarily an indication of quality, but there was so much at stake when the Miami Dolphins came up against the Kansas City Chiefs in the 1971 AFC playoffs that it seemed like it was destined to be a classic.

With the Chiefs going up 10-0 in the first quarter, the Dolphins responded in kind during the second. Throughout the third and fourth they pushed each other to the limit, scoring touchdowns that came within a heartbeat of each other. This took the game into overtime, where even an intercepted pass courtesy of Dolphins safety Jake Scott couldn't break the Chiefs' defense down.

At 7:40 of the second overtime period, however, Miami kicker Garo Yepremian converted a field goal to secure the win. The time on the clock was 82 minutes and 40 seconds.

SCORE: Miami Dolphins 27 – 24 Kansas City Chiefs
GAME: AFC divisional playoff
DATE: 25 December 1971
VENUE: Municipal Stadium, Kansas City, MO

Tom Brady, Julian Edelman and David Andrews celebrate pulling off the most unlikely of victories

THE COMEBACK TO END ALL COMEBACKS

10 **28-3 is a scoreline that will haunt every Atlanta Falcons fan until the end of their days.** 28-3 was the score, in the Falcons' favour, with a little over two minutes left of the third quarter in Super Bowl LI. The New England Patriots had been unable to contain the rampant Atlanta offense, led by league MVP Matt Ryan, and were staring defeat in the face.

At one point, Vegas had the Falcons' chances of winning at 99.8 per cent. Three teams had previously overcome a deficit of 10 points to win a Super Bowl – the Patriots had done it themselves in 2015 – but 25? It wasn't just improbable, it was unthinkable, laughable. It shouldn't have been possible.

Not for Bill Belichick's Pats team. Not for Tom Brady. A pair of James White touchdowns, a Danny Amendola score, a Stephen Gostkowski field goal and one breathtaking Julian Edelman catch later, and the scores were level. For the first time ever, the Super Bowl would be decided in overtime.

From that point on, the outcome was inevitable. Brady and White combined to produce a 75-yard drive, and the latter ran in his third touchdown of the night to clinch victory. It was the first time the Patriots had led the game.

Super Bowl LI set records which, in all likelihood, will stand for decades. It might still be fresh in the memory, but it's already reached mythic status. Few would argue against it as the greatest game in the history of the NFL.

SCORE: New England Patriots 34 - 28 Atlanta Falcons
GAME: Super Bowl LI
DATE: 5 February 2017
VENUE: NRG Stadium, Houston, TX

Walter Payton of the Chicago Bears
carrying the ball against the
Washington Redskins during the 1980s

50 ICONIC NFL PLAYERS

We assemble some of the most influential players to ever grace the National Football League and find out exactly what it was that made them so special

To succeed in a gruelling sport like football requires a fistful of traits that can't be coached. Athletic ability and/or a frame that can stop a locomotive in its tracks are a given, but beyond that the sport requires guile, mental strength and the ability to get inside the head of your opponents. Needless to say, the sport has thrown up many great players over the years that have these skills in abundance, and here we showcase some of the greatest individuals to ever grace the gridiron field.

From laser-guided ball throwers to rapier-like runners, immovable linebackers to unflappable receivers, there is no shortage of legends to take up any position on the pitch. And while there are hundreds, maybe even thousands of players worthy of a place in this list, we have tried to present a wide range of candidates, some of whom were incredible at what they did, and others who had the oversized personalities to match their status on the pitch. So, from the players employed to win games to those there to prevent the opposition from doing so, whatever the cost, here is our list of 50 of the NFL's most iconic players.

JOHNNY UNITAS

01 Spending the majority of his career with the Baltimore Colts, quarterback Johnny Unitas was voted the NFL's most valuable player in 1957, 1959, 1964 and 1967. For decades he held the record for the most consecutive games with a touchdown pass, which he set between 1956 and 1960, before he was finally surpassed by Drew Brees in 2012.

JOE GREENE

02 Greene played defensive tackle for the Pittsburgh Steelers throughout the early 1970s and was known as 'Mean Joe' Greene because of his no-nonsense approach to defending. Never afraid to steamroll his opponents, Greene was the winner of two NFL Defensive Player of the Year awards and the recipient of five first team All-Pro selections. He also won the Super Bowl four times in one of the most distinguished NFL careers of all time.

DARRELL GREEN

03 Considered to be one of the best cornerbacks to play in the NFL, Darrell Green spent his entire playing career (from 1983 to 2002) with the Washington Redskins and was famed for his considerable speed. Nicknamed the 'Ageless Wonder' by his peers for his energetic performances on the pitch well into the twilight of his career, Green was a two-time Super Bowl Champion (XXII and XXVI).

RONNIE LOTT

04 During his 14 seasons in the NFL (from 1981 to 1995), Ronnie Lott played cornerback, free safety and strong safety for the San Francisco 49ers, Los Angeles Raiders, New York Jets and the Kansas City Chiefs and was inducted into the Pro Football Hall of Fame in 2000. Widely considered to be one of the best safeties of all time, Lott recorded 85 sacks and 63 interceptions during his NFL career, which he returned for 730 yards and five touchdowns.

DON HUTSON

05 Spending 11 seasons with the Green Bay Packers from 1935 to 1945, Don Hutson was considered the game's first modern receiver and is credited with creating many of the pass routes that are still used in the NFL today. Back in his day, Hutson held all of the major records associated with wide receivers, including career receptions, yards and touchdowns, and although he played before the advent of the Super Bowl, he triumphed three times in the NFL Championship game that preceded it.

EMMITT SMITH

06 Spending the majority of his 15 seasons in the NFL with the Dallas Cowboys, running back Emmitt Smith became the league's all-time rushing leader with a total of 18,355 yards from 4,409 carries, breaking the previous record set by Walter Payton. Part of three Super Bowl-winning Cowboys teams, Smith also holds the unprecedented honour of being the only running back to win a Super Bowl championship, the NFL MVP, the NFL rushing crown and the Super Bowl MVP award in the same season (1993). In total he led the league in rushing and won the Super Bowl in the same year on three occasions (also in 1992 and 1995) and is one of only two non-kickers to score more than 1,000 NFL career points.

TERRY BRADSHAW

07 A veteran of 14 seasons for the Pittsburgh Steelers, Terry Bradshaw was the first quarterback to win three (1974, 1975 and 1978) and then four (1979) Super Bowls and led the Steelers to eight AFC Central championships. Robust, and with an arm that could launch a satellite into outer space, Bradshaw retired in 1983 with a record of 2,025 pass completions from 3,901 attempts, including 212 touchdown passes. Although that record equates to just a 51.9 per cent completion rating, it was Bradshaw's all-round performances, including his leadership on the field, that made him a Steelers legend. After football he got into acting and made several cameo appearances in films like *Smokey And The Bandit II*.

JOE SCHMIDT

08 If Schmidt's photo looks alarming enough then imagine the terror that he used to strike into the hearts of opposing offensive players when he faced them as linebacker for the Detroit Lions. A two-time NFL Champion (in 1953 and 1957) before the Super Bowl existed, Schmidt's toughness on and off the field meant that he bounced back quickly from injuries and his stopping abilities were recognised with ten Pro Bowl inclusions. When he retired in 1965, having spent 13 seasons playing with the Lions, Schmidt moved into a coaching role at the Lions before managing them two years later. He was inducted into the Pro Football Hall of Fame in 1973 and the College one in 2000.

MORTEN ANDERSEN

09 Born in Copenhagen (and so nicknamed 'The Great Dane'), Morten Andersen holds both the record for the most games played in the NFL (382) and the title of all-time leading scorer in NFL history. Not only that, but he's also the all-time leading scorer for two different teams – the New Orleans Saints and the Atlanta Falcons. First visiting the United States in 1977 as an exchange student, he so impressed as kicker for the Ben Davis High School team in Indianapolis that he was given a scholarship to Michigan State University. Famed for his bare-foot kicking style, Andersen kicked an outstanding 302 field goals for the Saints, including a 60-yarder against Chicago in 1991. He joined the Falcons in 1994 and became the first player to kick three field goals from over 50 yards in a game.

LARRY ALLEN

10 Regarded as one of the strongest men to have ever played professional football in the NFL (he recorded an official bench press of 705lbs and a squat of 905lbs), Larry Allen worked tirelessly as a guard for the Dallas Cowboys (1994-2005) and the San Francisco 49ers (2006-07). Recognised as one of the NFL's all-time greatest offensive linemen, Allen's physical might meant that he was able to play in most of the offensive line positions during his career. At various times, he played right tackle, right guard, left tackle and left guard, and he was also a victor at Super Bowl XXX when his Cowboys team triumphed over the Pittsburgh Steelers. Having spent 12 seasons with the Cowboys, Allen played his final two with the 49ers before returning to sign a one-day contract with Dallas so that he could retire with the team that drafted him.

WALTER PAYTON

11 Running back Walter Payton started his professional NFL career with the Chicago Bears in 1975 and remained at Soldier Field for 13 seasons. During that time, Payton held records for the most career rushing yards, touchdowns, carries, yards from scrimmage and more. He helped the Bears win Super Bowl XX against the New England Patriots in 1985 and also proceeded to pick up two NFL MVP awards in a career in which he amassed over 16,726 rushing yards. Payton's motto was 'Never Die Easy', which he put into practice during matches by not making it easy for his tacklers by deliberately running out of bounds before being tackled. He retired in 1987 and passed away in 1999.

ERIC DICKERSON

12 Spending 11 seasons in the NFL during the 1980s and 1990s as a running back, mainly for the Los Angeles Rams (but also with stints at the Indianapolis Colts, LA Raiders and Atlanta Falcons), Eric Dickerson holds the record for rushing in a single season with 2,105 yards, which he set in 1984.

After bursting onto the scene in 1983, Dickerson was the NFL rushing yards leader in his rookie season (in which he also picked up the NFL MVP and Rookie of the Year awards) and repeated the feat in 1984, 1986 and 1988. Unsurprisingly, his running exploits led to him being selected for six Pro Bowl appearances and making five All-Pro first teams during this purple patch. Throughout the course of his career, Dickerson amassed a total of 13,259 rushing yards, scoring 90 touchdowns in the process. The only thing lacking from his playing resumé is a Super Bowl winner's ring. As his career wound down, Dickerson appeared for other NFL teams, but he will mostly be remembered with the horns of the LA Rams emblazoned on the side of his helmet as he charged down the field.

GALE SAYERS

13 **Known in his playing days as 'The Kansas Comet', Gale Sayers spent seven seasons in the NFL as running back for the Chicago Bears during the 1960s and 1970s.** A member of the College Football Hall of Fame after his outstanding performances for the University of Kansas, Sayers was also inducted into the Pro Football Hall of Fame in 1977, and is still the youngest person to be inducted in the Hall's history. During his career, Sayers set records for the most touchdowns in a rookie season (22 in 1965), the most touchdowns scored in a single game (six), the highest career kickoff return average (30.56) and the most return touchdowns in a game (two). After retiring from the game, Sayers became a successful entrepreneur in information technology.

DERRICK BROOKS

15 **After playing for Florida State University, linebacker Derrick Brooks was drafted by the Tampa Bay Buccaneers in the first round of the 1995 draft and went on to spend his entire 14-season professional career there.** During his time with the Buccaneers, Brooks made 1,715 tackles, 13.5 quarterback sacks and 25 interceptions. He also pitched in on the scoresheet on occasion by scoring seven touchdowns – a respectable return for someone employed to stop the other team from scoring.

His immoveability as a linebacker meant that Brooks was selected for the Pro Bowl 11 times and voted as an All-Pro (one of the best players in his position as voted for by sports writers) on nine occasions. He was also named All-Pro NFL Defensive Player of the Year in 2002 and helped the Buccaneers win Super Bowl XXXVII in 2003 when they defeated the Oakland Raiders. Brooks retired from playing in 2008.

MARCUS ALLEN

14 **Allen was a mercurial talent on the gridiron field and played mainly as a running back for the Los Angeles Raiders (from 1982 to 1992) and the Kansas City Chiefs (from 1993 to 1997).** Considered one of the best goal line and short-yard runners in NFL history, Allen rushed for a total of 12,243 yards over his career, caught 587 passes for a total of 5,412 yards and scored 145 touchdowns. He was also pretty handy at passing, completing 12 of 27 passes for 285 yards and six touchdowns. Allen won one Super Bowl (XVIII) in 1983.

MIKE SINGLETARY

16 So integral was Mike Singletary to the defensive line of the famous Super Bowl-winning Chicago Bears side of the mid-1980s that he was actually nicknamed 'The Heart of the Defense'. Singletary remained with the Bears throughout his entire playing career (from 1981 to 1992) and racked up a phenomenal 1,488 crunching tackles, 19 crucial quarterback sacks and seven interceptions. Inducted into the Pro Football Hall of Fame in 1999, Singletary moved into coaching after retiring from playing and was linebacker coach for the Baltimore Ravens and San Francisco 49ers before getting the main coaching gig at the latter. Unfortunately, he was then relieved of his position with one game remaining of the 2010 season. He still coaches today, and presumably never has to buy his own drinks in Chicago.

JOE NAMATH

17 Quarterback Namath began his professional NFL career with the New York Jets in 1965 and spent 11 seasons with them before finishing off his playing days with one season at the Los Angeles Rams. A victor in Super Bowl III, Namath threw 173 touchdowns and completed 1,886 passes for 27,663 yards during his career. While these stats aren't exceptional, he was still inducted into the Pro Football Hall of Fame and, during his playing days, Namath became the NFL's first real media superstar, something that would serve him well after he retired from pro football and moved into acting. He has appeared in numerous TV shows since the late 1970s, and is one of many sports stars immortalised in *The Simpsons*.

EARL CAMPBELL

18 Earl Campbell was the running back with the Houston Oilers who exploded onto the scene in 1978 when he led the NFL in rushing in each of his first three seasons – becoming the only player ever to do so. In his third season in the NFL, Campbell rushed for over 200 yards in four separate games, which is a record that still stands today. Staying with the Oilers until 1984, he had one season with the New Orleans Saints before retiring in 1985. His considerable talent couldn't yield a Super Bowl winner's ring, but he did appear in five Pro Bowls and received numerous other awards, including the NFL Most Valuable Player (three times), NFL Offensive Player of the Year (three times) and many more during a distinguished career.

TONY GONZALEZ

19 A durable tight end for the Kansas City Chiefs and the Atlanta Falcons, Tony Gonzalez only missed two games during his entire 17-year NFL career. He also currently holds the NFL records for the most pass receptions (1,325), touchdown receptions (111) and total receiving yards (15,127) for a player in his position. In fact, following the start of the 2000 season, Gonzalez made 1,145 receptions with only one fumble, making him one of the safest pair of hands in NFL history. He was selected for 14 Pro Bowls and six All-Pro first teams during his career and after retiring from the game back in 2013 he made an effortless transition into football analysis and punditry – most recently moving from CBS to FOX's NFL Kickoff pregame show.

JIM BROWN

20 This fullback fittingly spent his entire career with the Cleveland Browns, from 1957 to 1965. Brown was the first player to reach 100 rushing touchdowns (which only a handful of players have done since) and his record of 100 touchdowns scored in 93 games stood until 2006.

JIM KELLY

21 With his no-huddle, 'K-Gun' offensive style, quarterback Jim Kelly led the Buffalo Bills to a record four consecutive Super Bowls from 1991 to 1994. Although they agonisingly lost all of them, Kelly was inducted into the Pro Football Hall of Fame in 2002.

PATRICK MAHOMES

23 Probably the best player currently active in the game, Mahomes was selected by the Kansas City Chiefs in 2017 and spent his first season backing up Alex Smith. But when he was handed the reins at the start of his second season, he quickly proved to be a star. He passed for 5,000 yards and 50 touchdowns, helping him be named MVP. The following year, Mahomes led the Chiefs to Super Bowl success, and he won his second ring in 2022. Kansas City made it to the AFC Championship game in every one of Mahomes' first five seasons as starter, making them the NFL's new dynasty.

LADAINIAN TOMLINSON

22 Identifiable from the dark visor he wore over the grid of his helmet to combat a sensitivity to light, LaDainian Tomlinson spent the majority of his 11-year NFL career as running back for the San Diego Chargers (from 2001-2009) before finishing at the New York Jets (2010-2011). He amassed a total of 13,684 rushing yards, scoring 145 touchdowns with his standout season coming in 2006 when he set several touchdown scoring records and received numerous honours, including the NFL's Most Valuable Player award.

ART SHELL

24 **As a no-nonsense offensive tackle for the Oakland/Los Angeles Raiders, Art Shell holds the distinction of becoming only the second-ever African-American head coach in the history of pro football when he took over the reigns of his beloved Raiders after hanging up his boots in 1983.** As a player, Shell played in 24 playoff contests and was on the winning side at Super Bowls XI and XV.

His hard-hitting exploits on the field were rewarded with eight call-ups for the Pro Bowl and he also featured in the NFL 1970s All-Decade Team. After moving into coaching, Shell won the Super Bowl again as coach of the Raiders when he masterminded their obliteration of the Washington Redskins at Super Bowl XVIII. He was also named NFL Coach of the Year in 1990. After leaving the Raiders in 1995, Shell also coached the Atlanta Falcons for three seasons before returning to manage the Raiders again in 2006, although this time the outcome was far from pleasing for both parties – he led the team to its worst record (of two wins and 14 defeats) since 1963. Shell was elected to the Pro Football Hall of Fame in 1989 and in 1999 he was ranked number 55 on The Sporting News' list of the 100 Greatest Football Players.

DAN MARINO

25 **Despite never being on a Super Bowl-winning team, Dan Marino is still recognised as being one of the greatest quarterbacks in NFL history.** Fondly remembered for his quick release and powerful throwing arm, he spent his entire playing career (from 1983 to 1999) with the Miami Dolphins. Marino was the NFL's leader in passing yards from 1984 to 1986 – and also in the 1988 and 1992 seasons – and the touchdown passing leader from 1984-1986. Synonymous with the number 13 jersey (which the Dolphins retired in his honour), Marino threw a then-NFL record of 48 touchdown passes in only his second season, when the Dolphins got all the way to, and lost, Super Bowl XIX.

STEVE YOUNG

26 A quarterback for the Tampa Bay Buccaneers and the 49ers, Young won a record six NFL passer rating titles, and at the time of his retirement from football he had the highest passer rating in the NFL with 96.8 per cent completion over 1,500 attempts.

MIKE DITKA

27 'Iron' Mike Ditka is one of the few people to win a Super Bowl as a player, assistant coach and head coach. He managed these feats during his time with the Dallas Cowboys and the Chicago Bears. Bringing new versatility to the tight end position, Ditka was a potent offensive player, as well as offering plenty of robust blocking.

WILLIAM PERRY

28 Perry was a bruising defensive lineman with the Bears and the Eagles. His size (standing 6ft2in tall and weighing 335lbs) earned him the nickname 'The Refrigerator' and he became one of the most recognisable faces (or builds) in the sport.

JERRY RICE

29 Widely considered to be the greatest wide receiver in NFL history, Jerry Rice played an incredible 20 seasons in the league, mainly for the San Francisco 49ers, but also for the Oakland Raiders and the Seatle Seahawks. Retiring in 2004, Rice is still the all-time leader in most wide receiver-related statistics, including pass receptions (1,540), touchdown receptions (197) and receiving yards (22,895).

Rice was a Super Bowl winner on three occasions with the 49ers and, after stints at the Raiders and Seahawks, he declined an initial one-year contract from the Denver Broncos at the end of the 2004 season, instead signing a one-day contract with the 49ers to allow him to retire as a member of the team where he began his career. Rice played 303 games in total, missing only 17 regular season games in his 20 professional seasons and was inducted into the Pro Football Hall of Fame in 2010 in his first year of eligibility. The 49ers have since retired the number 80 jersey in his honour.

TROY AIKMAN

30 Quarterback Troy Aikman spent his entire playing career (from 1989 to 2000) with the Dallas Cowboys, and during this illustrious period he was selected for the Pro Bowl six times and led his team to three Super Bowl victories. He was named MVP at Super Bowl XXVII when his Dallas team trounced the Buffalo Bills.

Aikman was at the peak of his powers in the early 1990s, and in 1992 he set career highs in pass completions (302), passing yards (3,445) and touchdown passes (23) while leading the Cowboys to a team-record 13 victories in the regular season – the second best record in the NFC.

A magnet for heavy hits, Aikman was seemingly regularly struck down with concussion (he claims to remember very little about his Super Bowl XXVIII victory) and he was rotated with former Philadelphia Eagles quarterback, Randall Cunningham. However, a persistent back injury eventually forced him to retire at the end of the 2000 season.

MICHAEL IRVIN

31 Nicknamed 'The Playmaker' due to his penchant for making big plays in big games, Michael Irvin was a wide receiver for the Dallas Cowboys from 1988 to 1999. Throughout a glittering playing career, Irvin won the Super Bowl three times (XXVII, XXVIII and XXX) and made 750 pass receptions over 11,904 yards, while also scoring 65 touchdowns. His career was ended during a game against the Philadelphia Eagles when he landed headfirst into the turf and suffered a serious spinal injury. Since retiring he has carved out a career in the sports media and has also appeared in several films, such as the 2005 remake of *The Longest Yard* starring Adam Sandler.

TONY DORSETT

33 A running back for the Dallas Cowboys and the Denver Broncos, Tony Dorsett's NFL career began in 1977. He would go on to become a legend with the Cowboys, winning the NFL Offensive Rookie of the Year award in his first season and racking up over 12,000 rushing yards in his 11 seasons with the franchise. One of his defining moments came in a game against the St Louis Cardinals in 1980 when, on the four-yard line, he displayed some unbelievably fancy footwork to elude five hapless defenders and carry the football into the end zone without being touched, resulting in one of his 92 career touchdowns.

BRUCE MATTHEWS

32 An offensive tackle for the NFL's Oilers/Titans franchise, Bruce Matthews played offensive tackle for 19 seasons from 1983 to 2001 and comes from a football dynasty. His father, Clay Matthews Sr played in the NFL in the 1950s, and his brother, Clay Matthews Jr, played in the NFL for the Cleveland Browns at the same time as Bruce. What's more, Bruce is the uncle of the Green Bay Packers linebacker Clay Matthews III, Minnesota Vikings linebacker Casey Matthews and even his sons now play professional football for various teams – it must be in the blood. During his own career, Bruce was selected for 14 Pro Bowls, was included in the NFL's All-Decade team for the 1990s and had the honour of having his number 74 jersey retired by the Tennessee Titans when he stopped playing.

FRAN TARKENTON

34 In a career stretching from 1961 to 1978, Fran Tarkenton served as quarterback for the Minnesota Vikings and the New York Giants. Picked by the Vikings in the third round of the 1961 NFL Draft, in his first game Tarkenton came off the bench with his team trailing to the Chicago Bears and passed for 250 yards (including four touchdown passes) and rushed for a touchdown of his own to complete an unlikely comeback. He was the NFL's passing yards leader in 1978, made nine Pro Bowl appearances and picked up countless other awards in a career that ended with the Vikings retiring his number 10 jersey.

NORM VAN BROCKLIN

35 Nicknamed 'The Dutchman', Norm Van Brocklin played as a quarterback (and occasional punter) for the Los Angeles Rams and the Philadelphia Eagles during the 1950s.

An accurate passer of the ball, Van Brocklin's career passing rating was 75.1, a stat that saw him selected for the Pro Bowl nine times and be awarded the NFL's MVP award in 1960.

After retiring from playing, Van Brocklin moved into coaching and had stints coaching the Minnesota Vikings and Atlanta Falcons. He is fondly remembered as one of the game's more colourful personalities.

ED REED

36 Picked by the Baltimore Ravens in the first round of the 2002 draft, defensive back Ed Reed played there for 11 seasons before joining the Houston Texans and then the New York Jets. He ultimately signed a one-day contract, as is quite common for legendary-status players, back at the Ravens to retire as a member of their squad. During his playing career, Reed made 643 tackles, 64 interceptions (returning them for a total of 1,590 yards – an all-time NFL record) and scored an incredible 13 touchdowns.

Reed was voted the NFL Defensive Player of the Year in 2004 and was selected in a total of nine Pro Bowls. Such was his professionalism that he was known to meticulously study films of his opposing teams to memorise their tendencies, and he was also noted for his ability to lure quarterbacks into making ill-judged passes that could be intercepted. After retiring from playing, Reed joined the Buffalo Bills as assistant defensive backs coach, leaving in 2016 when the coaching team was replaced. He has since been courted by a number of other franchises and linked with a return to the Ravens.

ELROY HIRSCH

37 Known affectionately as 'Crazylegs' on account of his unusual running style, Elroy Hirsch was a well-known running back and receiver for the Los Angeles Rams and Chicago Rockets. Never heard of the Rockets? Well, this was back in the 1940s. Born in Wisconsin to German-Norwegian parents, Hirsch was drafted by the Rockets in 1946 and spent three injury-prone seasons in Chicago before moving to the Rams in 1949. It was in LA that Hirsch become famous, and he was one of the first players to wear the moulded plastic helmet that is now the industry standard. When playing for the Rockets, on one occasion he was tackled so severely that he tore his right knee ligaments and actually fractured his skull just above his right ear. So, when he eventually moved to the Rams, his coach fitted him for the helmet as a precaution.

Elroy Hirsch was pivotal to the Rams' 1951 NFL Championship-winning season with a record 1,495 yards receiving, which stood for the next 19 years, as well as 66 catches and 17 touchdowns in 12 games. He was inducted into the Pro Football Hall of Fame in 1968 having racked up 387 receptions for 7,029 yards and 60 touchdowns across his playing career. After retiring, Hirsch became the director of athletics at the University of Wisconsin-Madison, raising home attendance at their football games overnight.

ANTHONY MUÑOZ

38 Widely considered to be one of the NFL's greatest ever offensive linemen, Anthony Muñoz played 13 seasons for the Cincinnati Bengals from 1980 to 1992. At the time of his retirement, Muñoz was tied with Tom Mack for the most ever Pro Bowl appearances by an offensive lineman and was the highest ranked lineman (at 17) when the Sporting News compiled its list of the 100 greatest football players. Muñoz also appeared in two motion pictures, one being 1983's *The Right Stuff*, which was nominated for an Academy Award.

PEYTON MANNING

39 Quarterback Peyton Manning played for an incredible 18 seasons in the NFL – 14 with the Indianapolis Colts and four with the Denver Broncos. During that time he won the NFL MVP award five times and won the Super Bowl twice (once with each team). Coming from a rich dynasty of playmakers (his father was former Saints quarterback Archie Manning and his brother, Eli, is the current quarterback for the New York Giants), Peyton Manning's career stats rank him up there with the very best to have played the game.

During his time with the Colts, Manning led them to eight division championships, two AFC championships and a Super Bowl championship (triumphing over the Chicago Bears at Super Bowl XLI). His five NFL MVP awards are a league record and he was named in 14 Pro Bowls, largely thanks to his 14 successful 4,000-yard passing seasons – which is also an NFL record. In winning Super Bowl 50 in his final game, Manning also became the first quarterback to achieve 200 career wins.

OJ SIMPSON

41 Before the shocking crimes that would come to define his image, the man nicknamed 'The Juice' was a prolific running back for the Buffalo Bills from 1969 to 1977, and was the first running back to rush more than 2,000 yards in a season. Although six other players have since passed this rushing landmark, OJ is the only person to have done it in a 14-game season (the NFL changed the format to a 16-game season in 1978). In total, Simpson's career haul of 11,236 rushing yards meant that he retired in 1979 placed second on the NFL's all-time list (he has since slipped to 18th). He also appeared in six Pro Bowls.

JOE MONTANA

40 Few NFL quarterbacks can boast as influential a record as Joe Montana. Starting his career with the San Francisco 49ers in 1979, Montana spent 14 seasons with the west-coast team, guiding them to four Super Bowl victories and becoming the first player to ever be named Super Bowl Most Valuable Player three times. He also holds Super Bowl career records for the most passes without an interception (122 in four games) and holds the all-time highest quarterback rating of 127.8. He was a constant performer who relished the big games and was noted for his calmness under pressure, leading to one of his two nicknames of 'Joe Cool'.

With his ice-cool demeanour, Montana also earned the second of his nicknames, 'The Comeback Kid' thanks to his ability to dig deep and fashion wins for his team by coming from behind in the fourth quarter of no less than 31 games throughout his career, most notably at Super Bowl XXIII. With his team trailing to the Cincinnati Bengals, Montana orchestrated an incredible 92-yard drive that resulted in the game-winning touchdown for the 49ers with only 36 seconds left on the clock. One of the true legends of the field.

LAWRENCE TAYLOR

42 Playing his entire professional career as a linebacker with the New York Giants (from 1981-1993), Lawrence Taylor produced double-figure sack statistics in each season from 1984 to 1990. This run included a career-best of 20.5 in 1986, the year that he won his first of two Super Bowl titles with the Giants. That year, Taylor also became the first defensive player in history to win the NFL Most Valuable Player (MVP) award. Such was Taylor's immense standing in the game that not even suspensions for substance abuse could tarnish his reputation as one of the best defensive players to ever grace the NFL.

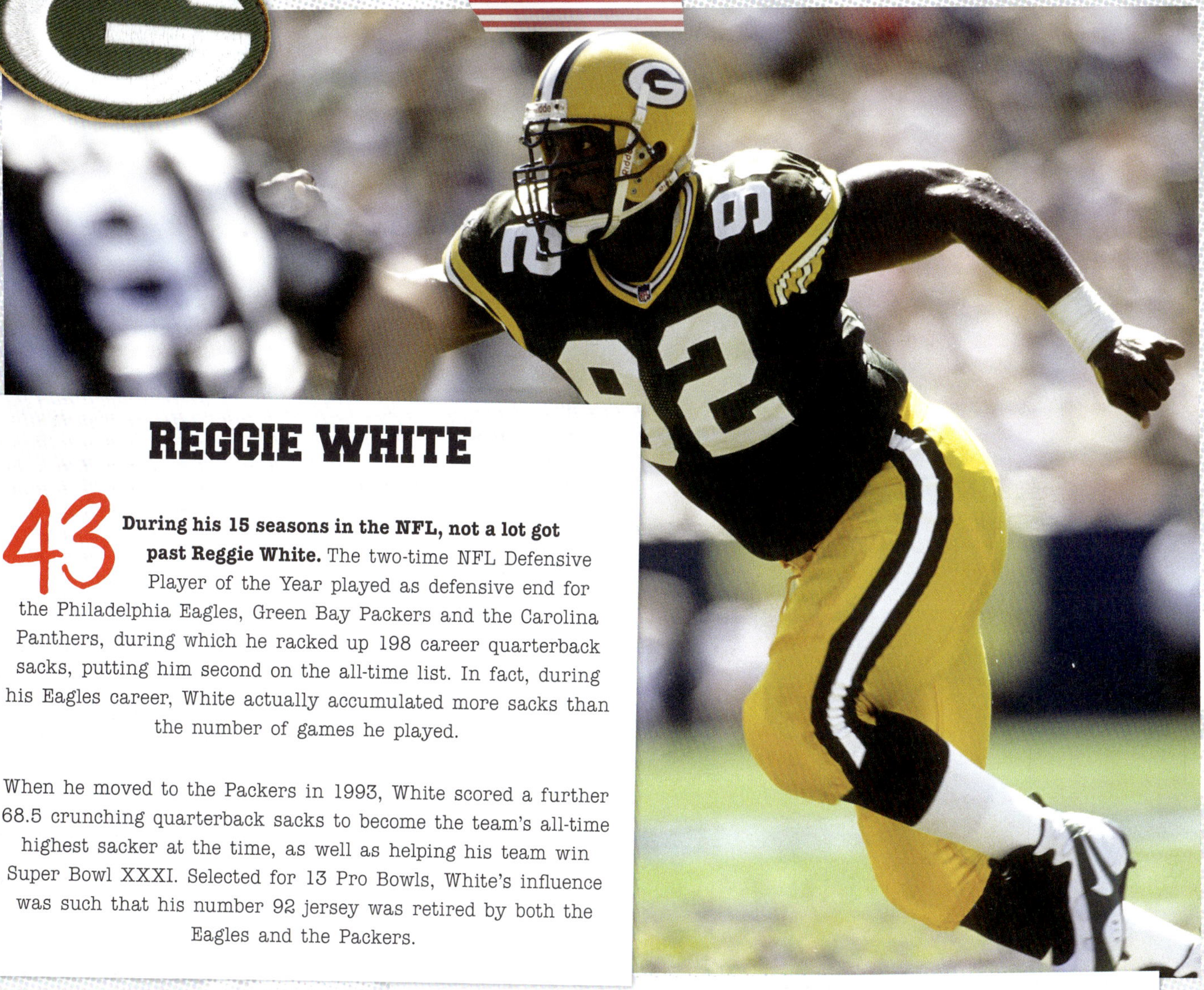

REGGIE WHITE

43

During his 15 seasons in the NFL, not a lot got past Reggie White. The two-time NFL Defensive Player of the Year played as defensive end for the Philadelphia Eagles, Green Bay Packers and the Carolina Panthers, during which he racked up 198 career quarterback sacks, putting him second on the all-time list. In fact, during his Eagles career, White actually accumulated more sacks than the number of games he played.

When he moved to the Packers in 1993, White scored a further 68.5 crunching quarterback sacks to become the team's all-time highest sacker at the time, as well as helping his team win Super Bowl XXXI. Selected for 13 Pro Bowls, White's influence was such that his number 92 jersey was retired by both the Eagles and the Packers.

RAY LEWIS

44

Considered one of the greatest linebackers of all time, Lewis began his NFL career with the Baltimore Ravens in 1996 (in the team's inaugural season) and stayed with them for his entire 17-year playing stretch in the league. During his playing days the accolades rained like confetti and Lewis was selected for 13 Pro Bowls, named as an Associated Press All-Pro ten times, won the NFL Defensive Player of the Year award twice and was also only the second ever linebacker to win the Super Bowl MVP award (the first to win it on the winning team) when the Ravens triumphed at Super Bowl XXXV in 2000.

During that season, Lewis led a water-tight defense that set a 16-game single-season record for the fewest points allowed (165) and the fewest rushing yards allowed (970) – he was a hard man to get around. After an unfortunate triceps tear sidelined him for a large proportion of the 2012-13 season, Lewis returned just in time for the Ravens' playoff run that extended all the way to Super Bowl XLVII, where they triumphed over the San Francisco 49ers.

DICK BUTKUS

45 Widely regarded as one of the best and most durable linebackers of all time, Dick Butkus played nine seasons in the NFL (from 1965-73) for the Chicago Bears and intimidated opposing players with this size and hard-hitting tackling ability. Though he never appeared at the Super Bowl, Butkus' defensive prowess was recognised with eight Pro Bowl appearances and two NFL Defensive Player of the Year awards. After retiring, Butkus moved into acting and some people may remember him more for appearances in Murder She Wrote and Magnum PI than his antics on the pitch. But for older Bears fans and those who appreciate a crunching tackle, Butkus will always be an NFL legend.

JOHN ELWAY

47 For a time during the late 1980s, it looked as though John Elway, the quarterback for the Denver Broncos would always be the bridesmaid and never the bride. After trips to Super Bowl XXI, XXII and XXIV, Elway finished on the losing team every time and despite being a consistent performer, it would take a dramatic slump in his team's fortunes and something of a rebirth before his talent would yield the ultimate prize.

Spending his entire 16-year career with the Broncos, Elway clocked up an impressive array of records before retiring in 1999. But it was a particular play during an AFC championship game against the Cleveland Browns in 1987 that proved to be his defining moment on the field. Elway helped to engineer a 98-yard game-tying touchdown drive that propelled the Broncos to Super Bowl XXI against the New York Giants. The Broncos would, crushingly, lose that game but Elway did eventually become a double champion at Super Bowls XXXII and XXXIII.

BART STARR

46 The modern NFL's first celebrity, the aptly named Starr became the first quarterback to win a Super Bowl when he lead the Packers to victory over the Chiefs. He then went on to repeat the feat a year later, being named MVP on both occasions. Over a 15-year playing career, Starr remained loyal to Green Bay, delivering five championships – a feat not equalled until 2017. Though his coaching career was less successful, it didn't take any of the shine off his playing achievements. Starr became a Hall of Famer in 1977, and the Packers have retired his number 15 jersey.

DEION SANDERS

48 **Sanders played a range of positions for a host of different NFL teams.** In stints with the Atlanta Falcons, San Francisco 49ers, Dallas Cowboys, Washington Redskins and Baltimore Ravens, he played cornerback, kick returner, punt returner and wide receiver. Amazingly, to further highlight Sanders' 'all-rounder' status, he also managed to balance a parallel sporting career and played baseball professionally for the New York Yankees, Atlanta Braves, Cincinnati Reds and the San Francisco Giants. He is still the only man to play in both a Super Bowl (winning Super Bowl XXIX with the 49ers and XXX with the Cowboys) and a World Series (with the Braves in 1992). In 1994, the same year he won the Super Bowl with the San Francisco 49ers, he was voted Defensive Player of the Year.

BRETT FAVRE

49 **Over his long and distinguished playing career, Favre's stats place him up there with the NFL's very best quarterbacks.** He was the first quarterback to complete over 6,000 passes, throw for over 70,000 yards and pass for 500 touchdowns. Drafted by the Atlanta Falcons in 1991, Favre was traded to the Green Bay Packers in 1992 and seized his opportunity to impress after an injury ruled out the Packers' starting quarterback, Don 'Majik Man' Majkowski. Incredibly, he then started every game for the Packers through to the end of the 2007 season and, subsequently, for the New York Jets and Minnesota Vikings to take his consecutive starts record to 321 (including playoff matches). Favre has led his teams to eight division championships and two Super Bowls (XXXI and XXXII), the first of which he won when the Packers defeated the New England Patriots.

TOM BRADY

50 **If there were any lingering doubts over Tom Brady's status as the greatest quarterback of all time, the result of Super Bowl LV surely put them to rest.** Brady's critics previously claimed that he only won because he was the central figure in Bill Belichick's New England team. But after Brady chose to depart the Patriots and end his career with the Tampa Bay Buccaneers, he instantly turned around the fortunes of a failing team and led them to Super Bowl success. With seven Super Bowls wins to his name, Brady doesn't just hold more rings than any other player – he has more titles than any other team. Starting his career in 2000, Brady holds multiple league MVP and Super Bowl MVP awards and his Patriots team holds the record for the longest consecutive winning streak, with a remarkable 21 wins spanning the 2003 and 2004 seasons. He also holds the record for the most consecutive playoff wins with ten and, in 2007, led the Patriots to the first undefeated regular season since the schedule was expanded to 16 games.

10 GREATEST NFL COACHES

It isn't just the number of wins that determines a coach's greatness, it is the creativity behind the science of drawing up the Xs and Os

The NFL's roots are based within the collegiate game. Grambling's Eddie Robinson was college football's all-time winning coach when he surpassed Bear Bryant's 323 wins, but he will be remembered for his ability to exert a positive influence on his players. Likewise, Knute Rockne's words, meticulous practices and his 'Four Horsemen' of Notre Dame mean he would be held among the greatest coaches of all time.

Aside for Walter Camp, who was the 'Father of American Football' and invented such things as the line of scrimmage, Amos Alonzo Stagg was the most important figure in the development of American Football, since he developed the rules. Few have done as much to popularise the game. Yet the following top ten coaches are from the professional ranks, who owe much to their predecessors.

This list is not necessarily about the number of wins achieved, it is about invention and creativity, minds from whom so much is copied or reinvented in the modern NFL. Let the arguments begin...

Jubilant Green Bay Packer players
give coach Vince Lombardi the
traditional victory ride

PRO FOOTBALL
HALL OF FAME

VINCE LOMBARDI
COACH

SWELL

Vince Lombardi is memorialised
by the Lombardi Trophy, awarded to
the winner of the Super Bowl

VINCE LOMBARDI

The man who built a Green Bay dynasty

01 Vince Lombardi never said, "Winning isn't everything; it is the only thing," although that is the quote most often attributed to him. His actual words were: "Winning is not everything, but making the effort to win is."

Shaped by family, religion and sports, the son of an Italian immigrant butcher, Lombardi was deeply influenced by the Jesuits, who taught him the philosophy he later used with his players, subordinating individual desires for the team ethic.

A guard on Fordham University's 'Seven Blocks of Granite' line in the mid-1930s, Lombardi did not play in the NFL, and instead went directly into coaching. From a High School coach in New Jersey, then as an assistant at Fordham, he progressed to West Point and then with the New York Giants under offensive coach Jim Lee Howell.

Known as Mr. High-Low, Lombardi was a loud and emotional man, a devout Catholic who attended Mass each day, yet was a contradictory character, whose career took 20 years to reach a peak. When he went to Green Bay in 1958, the Packers were at their lowest. Yet Lombardi

quickly changed quarterback flop Paul Hornung into a star running back, nurtured Bart Starr into a brilliant quarterback, and drove the team mercilessly, emphasising execution, blocking and tackling, and urging his players to endure pain.

He was far from perfect. Before a game, at half-time and after a game, his players thought of Lombardi as a football genius, always anticipating what opponents would do. He made game-plans simple, discarding the immaterial to get the 15 plays that he knew would work. Yet he was not much of an in-game adjuster. Hornung thought his coach "wasn't worth a crap during the game. He was an observer, a Kibitzer."

Yet upon arrival in Wisconsin, the results were instantaneous. His 1959 team won seven of 12 games. In 1960, Green Bay took the division title and in 1961 and 1962 Lombardi's Packers won the NFL title. Two years after retooling, they won three consecutive championships in 1965, 1966 and 1967. In 1969, the Washington Redskins hired him, but he was stricken with cancer and died on September 3, 1970, aged 57.

Over a ten-year tenure, his overall winning percentage was 74%. No other coach comes remotely close to matching that figure.

DON CORYELL

Technician of modern passing attack

02

Don Coryell designed the 'passing tree' of receiving routes and was dubbed 'Air Coryell' because of his innovation in the passing attack. The use of pass-catching tight-ends meant that nickel and dime defenses became an every-game proposition. His San Diego Chargers teams led the league in passing yardage in six straight seasons between 1978 to 1983, and again in 1985. Mike Martz, the creator of 'The Greatest Show on Turf' Rams teams, based his prolific offense on Coryell's pass-first offense. Coach of the Year in 1974, he won back-to-back division titles with the Cardinals in 1974-75. His revolutionary style and unique vision helped quarterback Dan Fouts, tight-end Kellen Winslow and receiver Charlie Joiner all reach the Hall of Fame, and his Chargers teams went to the AFC title games in 1980 and 1981.

CARD No. HOF2

PRO FOOTBALL HALL OF FAME
CANTON, OHIO

DON CORYELL

Air Coryell landed in Canton, Ohio, in 2023. It's the name given to the passing system devised by Coryell as head coach of the Chargers from 1978-86. With motion and timing, it attacked all areas of the field. His teams led the league in passing all but two seasons, and Hall of Fame QB Dan Fouts won four passing titles.

PANINI

2023 PANINI – HALL OF FAME

Class of 2023

© 2023 Panini America, Inc. Produced in the USA.

SAN DIEGO CHARGERS

Coryell was well known for his innovations to football's passing offense

BUDDY RYAN
Innovator of 46 Defense

03

A master sergeant in the Army during the Korean War at the age of 18, Buddy Ryan knew how to lead. As a defensive assistant under Weeb Ewbank with the New York Jets in the late 1960s, Ryan began thinking of creative ways to rush the passer when he saw the effect that pressure had on Jets' quarterback Joe Namath. Ryan tinkered with what initially was a nickel defense, designed to stop the pass, when with the Vikings in the late 70s and when he went to Chicago, he named it the '46 Defense' in honour of safety Doug Plank, who wore the 46 jersey. The concept was to put Dan Hampton, the most difficult-to-block player, on the centre, and crowd the offense with six men on the line and eight or nine in the box. Ryan usually blitzed between six and eight defenders. It was a strategy way ahead of its time and he never produced a better unit in his 26 seasons as a coach than the 1985 Bears' Super Bowl-winning defense.

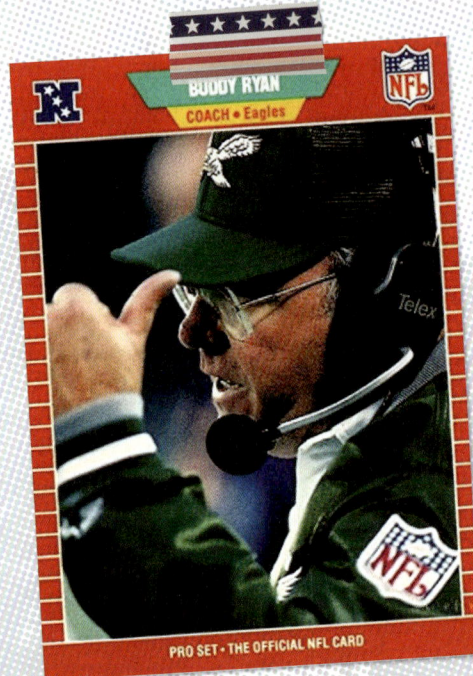

PRO SET · THE OFFICIAL NFL CARD

Ryan's sons, Rex and Rob, have both gone on to have coaching careers in the NFL

TOM LANDRY
Master of the Flex

04 **For the first 29 years of their existence, the Dallas Cowboys had only one head coach.** Tom Landry, a former standout with the University of Texas, was widely recognised as one of the sharpest defensive assistant coaches in the game in his four years with the New York Giants. It took him a few years to have a winning season after arriving in Dallas as head coach in 1960, yet the Cowboys posted 20 consecutive winning seasons between 1966-85 under Landry, who delivered 13 division championships, five NFC titles and Super Bowl victories in January 1972 and 1978 for 'America's Team'. He perfected the 'flex defense', a variation of the basic 4-3 alignment, took a page out of the San Francisco 49ers' playbook of the early 1960s when giving new life to the 'shotgun' formation, in which Cowboys quarterback Roger Staubach flourished, and embraced and developed the situational substitution, inserting players on certain downs for specific assignments.

Tom Landry's 270 career regular season win total is the third-highest ever recorded by an NFL coach

PAUL BROWN
Architect of film-study

05 **Like Vince Lombardi, Paul Brown would not win congeniality awards. He was all business when it came to football.** Yet he brought more innovation to the game than Lombardi. Brown introduced the practice of scientific study of films, intelligence tests for players, modern pass-blocking techniques, many new passing schemes and a 'messenger guard' system for sending in plays.

Brown, who played for the University of Miami (Ohio), had more cerebral talent than physical prowess. After two years at Seven Prep School as an assistant coach, he returned to his alma mater at Massillon, Ohio. Over nine seasons, his teams went 80-8-2 and won several state championships. In 1941, he became head coach at Ohio State and won the national championship in only his second year in Columbus. Hired after World War II as head coach of Cleveland's professional team in the newly-formed AFL, Brown produced a 47-4-3 record and four league titles. The Browns (a name selected in his honour from a 'name the team' newspaper contest) won four straight AAFC titles, then entered the NFL in 1950 and won the championship in their first year. In his first eight NFL seasons, the Browns won three league titles and seven division crowns. Fired in 1962 by Cleveland owner Art Modell after one losing season, he went back to pro football in 1968 as a founder and coach of the Cincinnati Bengals. With a roster of cast-offs, he won a division title in 1970 and repeated that in 1973.

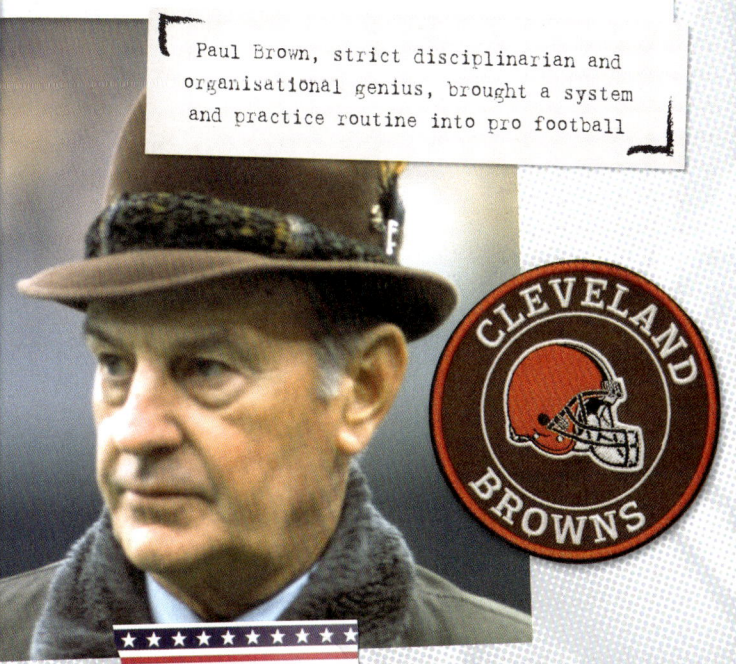

Paul Brown, strict disciplinarian and organisational genius, brought a system and practice routine into pro football

In 40 years of coaching George Halas compiled a 324-151-3 mark, second only to Don Shula

GEORGE HALAS
Mr. Everything

06 The Pro Football Hall of Fame sits on George Halas Drive. No address could be more appropriate, as Halas was pro football's 'Mr. Everything' as a founder, player and coach of the Chicago Bears. A charter member of both the NFL and the Pro Football Hall of Fame, Halas was a two-way end at Illinois, played pro football in 1919 in Chicago and, briefly, Major League Baseball with the New York Yankees. Hired by A. E. Staley to run his Decatur starch company's baseball and football teams, the Decatur Staleys joined as charter members of the first league in Canton in 1920. In 1921, Halas moved the Staleys to Chicago and won their first championship. The next year, he and partner Dutch Sternaman secured their own franchise, renaming the team the Chicago Bears, and in 1925 raised the profile of pro football by signing All-American Red Grange. Halas' greatest period came in the 1940s when his Bears won four league titles, with much of the success owing to the development of the modern 'T' formation, which quickly became a standard football offense. The Bears continue to wear his initials, 'GSH', on their sleeves to this day.

PRO FOOTBALL HALL OF FAME

Founder/Owner/Coach
GEORGE HALAS

DON SHULA
Born winner

07 **On November 14, 1993, when the Miami Dolphins defeated the Philadelphia Eagles 19-14, Don Shula became the greatest winning coach in NFL history.** His 325 career wins surpassed George Halas' record, and by the time he retired after 32 seasons, in 1995, he had a seemingly unmatchable 347 career wins. In 26 seasons with the Dolphins, he had one losing season. With the help of defensive coordinator Bill Arnsparger's 'no-name' defense, the Dolphins recorded the only perfect NFL season, going 17-0 in 1972. Longevity is what sets Shula's coaching career apart. It helped that his pro teams were led by three great quarterbacks, Johnny Unitas, Bob Griese and Dan Marino, and while his legacy is tarnished somewhat by a 19-17 post-season record, his consistent success is still the standard by which all NFL coaches will be measured.

> At 33, Don Shula became the youngest head coach in 1963 when taking over the Baltimore Colts

"The Dolphins recorded the only perfect NFL season, going 17-0 in 1972.

CHUCK NOLL
Founded a Pipeline of excellence

08 **He may have been considered distant, aloof and cold by some of those who played for him, but in the space of one decade, the intensely private and introspective Chuck Noll turned the doormat Pittsburgh Steelers, whom he joined at the age of 37 in 1969, from a two-win laughing stock into one of the NFL's premier franchises.** Noll was committed to drafting the right kind of players, with his focus purely on technique, preparation and detail. Within Noll's first five years, the Steelers drafted nine Hall of Fame players, including four in the 1974 draft, and with Bud Carson's Steel Curtain defense, they won back-to-back Super Bowls in 1974-75 and then again in 1978-79. Noll was not a rah-rah speaker. Players never got close to him. Indeed, L.C. Greenwood, a key defensive component for 13 years, only recalled having one conversation with Noll – the day he was cut from the team.

> Chuck Noll was a father figure, whose quiet leadership produced extraordinary results

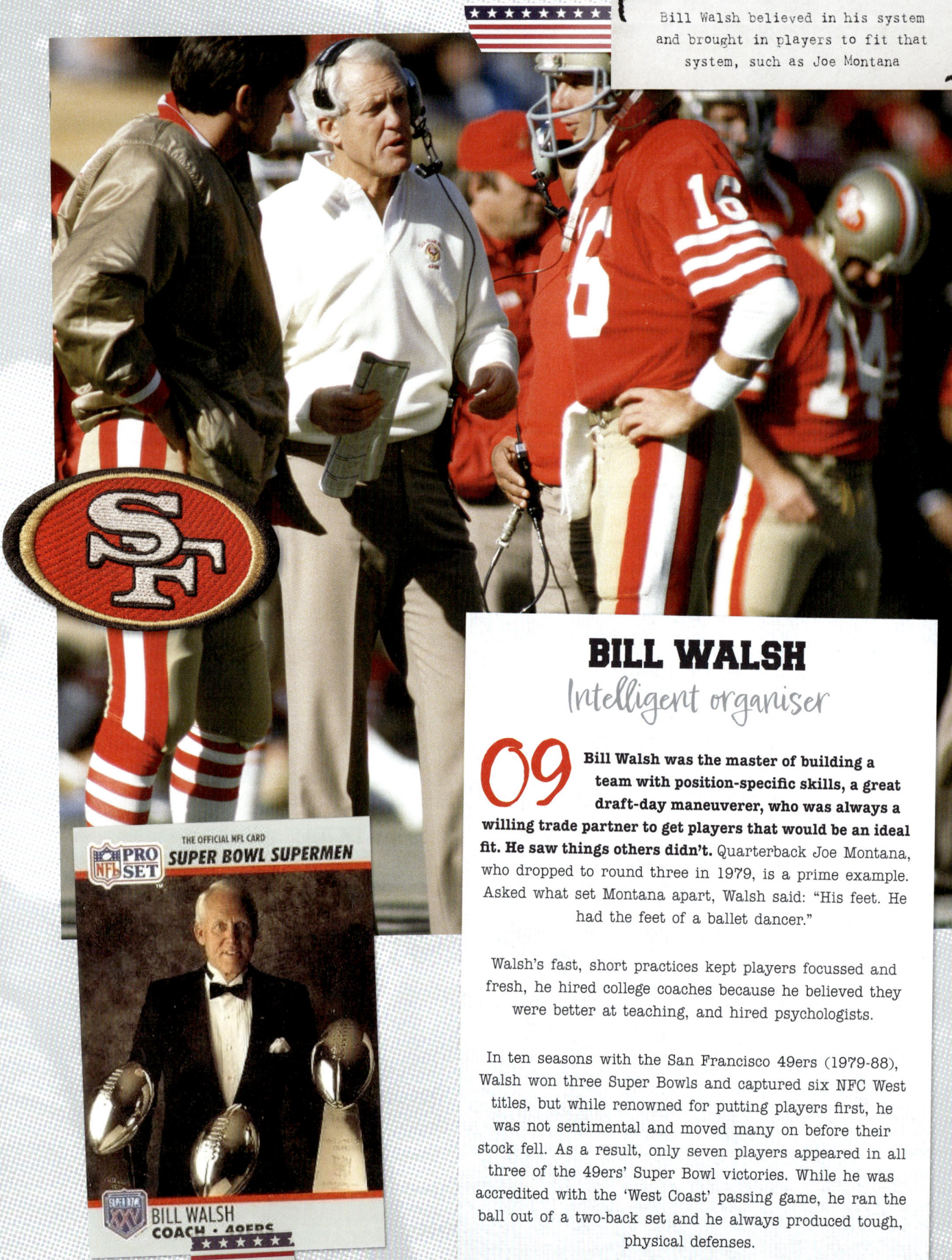

Bill Walsh believed in his system and brought in players to fit that system, such as Joe Montana

THE OFFICIAL NFL CARD
SUPER BOWL SUPERMEN

BILL WALSH
COACH · 49ERS

BILL WALSH
Intelligent organiser

09 **Bill Walsh was the master of building a team with position-specific skills, a great draft-day maneuverer, who was always a willing trade partner to get players that would be an ideal fit. He saw things others didn't.** Quarterback Joe Montana, who dropped to round three in 1979, is a prime example. Asked what set Montana apart, Walsh said: "His feet. He had the feet of a ballet dancer."

Walsh's fast, short practices kept players focussed and fresh, he hired college coaches because he believed they were better at teaching, and hired psychologists.

In ten seasons with the San Francisco 49ers (1979-88), Walsh won three Super Bowls and captured six NFC West titles, but while renowned for putting players first, he was not sentimental and moved many on before their stock fell. As a result, only seven players appeared in all three of the 49ers' Super Bowl victories. While he was accredited with the 'West Coast' passing game, he ran the ball out of a two-back set and he always produced tough, physical defenses.

Bill Belichick and Tom Brady have
built a dynasty in New England

BILL BELICHICK
The master recycler of talent

10 **Though he will defer the honour to Paul Brown, Bill Belichick's five Lombardi trophies and 28 post-season victories make him a front-runner in a small field for 'greatest NFL coach'.** No other head coach has achieved more Super Bowl wins. And he is the only coach on this list to still be plying his trade, having completed a eighth straight season in 2017 with at least 12 regular-season wins and a seventh straight appearance in the AFC Championship game. Having missed out on too many high-round picks, he is not a better draft builder than Bill Walsh, who was a savant at drafting the right players to fit. Yet Belichick has done a remarkable job in acquiring players that other teams gave up on too quickly, such as Wes Welker, Randy Moss, Aqib Talib and Corey Dillon. You can argue that NFL titles with New England in 2001, 2003, 2004, 2014 and 2016 put him in the pantheon of great coaches. But is he the best? The arguments rage on like no other.

Like other coaches, he had losing seasons before turning things around – in his case six as a head coach, including his time in Cleveland. A great coach is only as good as his quarterback, and Tom Brady fell into his lap in the sixth round in 2000. At the time Drew Bledsoe was injured and as Brady's stellar career began, Belichick was on the brink of being axed again. Where would Belichick be but for Brady?

> ***"No other head coach has achieved more Super Bowl wins"***

Arguably, the Patriots' dynasty may never have been created but for the leg of Adam Vinatieri, whose field goals were the deciding scores in their first three Lombardi trophies. And sadly, there is no denying the asterisk beside Belichick's career. In 2007, Spygate saw him fined $500,000 and the Patriots $250,000 for being caught videotaping opposing coaches, and evidence was found that it had been going on for years. Brady was also suspended for four games in 2015, and accused of deflating footballs in the AFC Championship game. There were accusations by the Rams that Belichick's staff spied on their walkthrough the night before Super Bowl XXXVII, and similar accusations came from Carolina GM Marty Hurney on the eve of Super Bowl XXXVIII.

While this may smack of jealousy, Belichick's legacy may yet end up tarnished by his own insatiable need to get an extra edge – by any means necessary.